"This book is both delightful and important. The style is so engaging that it is easy to overlook how rich it is in content. Not only do we learn a great deal about Lewis and Sayers but we are also treated to a nuanced account of the nature of *friendship* itself. I enjoyed every page of it, and I heartily recommend it. It is very, very good."

Diana Pavlac Glyer, professor at The Honors College, Azusa Pacific University; author of *The Company They Keep* and *Bandersnatch: C. S. Lewis, J. R. R. Tolkien, and the Creative Collaboration of the Inklings*

"I've read and enjoyed virtually everything by these two wonderful writers, but until now I'd never really fully understood the impact they had on each other. Gina's thoroughly researched and thoroughly entertaining book is filled with fresh insights about two of the greatest writers and most creative apologists of our time. If you are a fan of either writer, this is a book you'll want to read. It is simply a delight."

Terry Glaspey, author of *75 Masterpieces Every Christian Should Know, Not a Tame Lion: The Spiritual Legacy of C. S. Lewis,* and *The Prayers of Jane Austen*

"*Dorothy and Jack* is a enchanting gift, handcrafted with research, love, and intelligence. This book is about C. S. Lewis and Dorothy L. Sayers, but it is also about all of us; it is about the unexpected beauty in relationship. Dalfonzo's captivating narrative and profound understanding deepens and ultimately reveals the 'wild truth' of Dorothy and Jack—how they changed each other's lives, hearts, and work, and therefore how they have changed ours."

Patti Callahan, *New York Times* bestselling author of *Becoming Mrs. Lewis*

"Sadly, many readers of C. S. Lewis know little of Dorothy L. Sayers's works, and all too often the reverse is true as well. However, in *Dorothy and Jack*, Gina Dalfonzo has happily remedied this deficit by demonstrating the strong connections between these two Christian thinkers. *Dorothy and Jack* not only engagingly unfolds the deepening friendship between these two but also sheds welcome light on the significant value this friendship added to their lives. All those who love the writings of Sayers and Lewis will relish the insights and delight to be found in the pages of *Dorothy and Jack*."

Marjorie Lamp Mead, associate director of the Marion E. Wade Center, Wheaton College

"Dorothy Sayers is a required text for understanding and appreciating the works of both prodigious writers. Lewis and Sayers hailed from two very different worlds; however, Dalfonzo deftly illustrates how the two nurtured a lasting connection which thrived on humor, mutual respect, constructive criticism, and shared spiritual values. This book is a true gem."

Crystal Hurd, writer; poet; reviews editor
for *Sehnsucht: The C .S. Lewis Journal.*

"A well-researched and lively narrative like this one of the relationship between Dorothy L. Sayers and C. S. Lewis needed to be written. Dalfonzo has delved deeply into the history of both of these significant literary figures who also made their mark as apologists for the Christian faith. Her storytelling talent provides a vivid, attractive text that keeps the reader wanting to know more, and her analysis of the relationship is bracing and thought-provoking. One cannot ask for a better treatment of these Christian icons."

K. Alan Snyder, author of *America Discovers
C. S. Lewis: His Profound Impact*

"Much has been made of Lewis and his band of brothers. But the company of Tolkien, Barfield, Williams, and Dyson, while invaluable, offer something of a one-lensed view. I think we can still benefit from a clearer vision. Dalfonzo's work on Dorothy Sayers gives us a broader view than what the male monocle can offer. There's something in Lewis best seen through his relationship with Sayers—something formative, instructive, and encouraging—something transformational."

Corey Latta, author of *C. S. Lewis and the Art of Writing*

"As someone very familiar with Jack's life, I was surprised and pleased to learn more about the similarities between him and Sayers and how their differences impacted each other over the decade and a half they knew each other. Dalfonzo's work sheds much-needed light on this important friendship."

William O'Flaherty, author of *The Misquotable C .S. Lewis*;
creator of "90 Seconds to Knowing C. S. Lewis" on YouTube

"To pair Dorothy Sayers and Jack Lewis into one lucid, well-researched book is a tremendous contribution. *Dorothy and Jack* is an enjoyable read, especially for those who want a rigorous, unsentimental expression of orthodox Christianity within post-Christian culture."

Max McLean, artistic director of Fellowship for Performing Arts

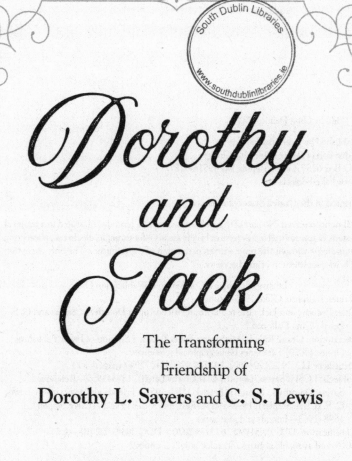

Dorothy and Jack

The Transforming
Friendship of
Dorothy L. Sayers and **C. S. Lewis**

GINA DALFONZO

BakerBooks
a division of Baker Publishing Group
Grand Rapids, Michigan

© 2020 by Gina Dalfonzo

Published by Baker Books
a division of Baker Publishing Group
PO Box 6287, Grand Rapids, MI 49516-6287
www.bakerbooks.com

Printed in the United States of America

Library of Congress Cataloging-in-Publication Data
Names: Dalfonzo, Gina, 1975– author.
Title: Dorothy and Jack : the transforming friendship of Dorothy L. Sayers and C. S. Lewis / Gina Dalfonzo.
Description: Grand Rapids, Michigan : Baker Books, a division of Baker Publishing Group, [2020] | Includes bibliographical references.
Identifiers: LCCN 2019046602 | ISBN 9780801072949 (paperback)
Subjects: LCSH: Sayers, Dorothy L. (Dorothy Leigh), 1893–1957—Religion. | Sayers, Dorothy L. (Dorothy Leigh), 1893–1957—Friends and associates. | Lewis, C. S. (Clive Staples), 1898–1963—Religion. | Lewis, C. S. (Clive Staples), 1898–1963—Friends and associates.
Classification: LCC BX5199.S267 D35 2020 | DDC 283.092/2 [B]—dc23
LC record available at https://lccn.loc.gov/2019046602

ISBN 978-1-5409-0092-0 (casebound)

In keeping with biblical principles of creation stewardship, Baker Publishing Group advocates the responsible use of our natural resources. As a member of the Green Press Initiative, our company uses recycled paper when possible. The text paper of this book is composed in part of post-consumer waste.

green press
INITIATIVE

For more than twenty-five years, they've consistently engaged my interest, expanded my horizons, cheered me up when I was down, inspired me when I felt weary and disillusioned, and strengthened my faith in my Savior and theirs. I consider them my mentors, teachers, and guides, even though I never had a chance to meet them.

To Dorothy L. Sayers and C. S. Lewis,
whose writings have done so much
to shape my thinking and my life,
this book is lovingly dedicated.

Contents

Introduction

They could not have been more alike.

Born five years apart in the waning years of the nineteenth century, both of them were favored, at least for a time, with the kind of idyllic British childhood you read about in classic children's stories.

Both were highly intelligent, perceptive, and creative from the start, developing a deep knowledge of and passion for literature. Both attended Oxford University, graduated with honors, and became famous writers of novels, essays, scholarly works, and more.

Each went through a period of spiritual rebellion in his or her youth but went on to become fruitful lifelong members of the Anglican church and respected Christian apologists with a theologically conservative bent.

They could not have been more different.

He lost his mother early and had a troubled relationship with his father. She had both of her parents in her life well into adulthood and was very close to them, though not always able to be as open with them as she would have liked to be.

9

Her marriage was strained; his marriage, though tragically short, was a very happy one.

His was generally a contented spirit, hers an adventurous, even reckless one. His manner was winsome if boisterous, hers just plain blunt. Much of what came naturally to her, in work and in life, was difficult for him, and vice versa.

Nevertheless, C. S. Lewis and Dorothy L. Sayers were friends for fifteen years—from the time she sent him a fan letter in 1942 until her death in 1957. It was a friendship that on one level caught fire quickly, as the two of them bonded over the many ideas, interests, and values they had in common, and yet took many years to deepen and intensify to the point where they were comfortable sharing their most personal struggles.

But all of those fifteen years were filled with correspondence, critiques, jokes, praise, cartoons, arguments, sympathy, and a true enjoyment of each other's company. Both of them complained about not being able to meet very often, as they were perpetually busy with their respective careers and family obligations, but the resulting benefit to us is the wonderful collection of letters they produced between them. Lewis told Sayers that she was "one of the great English letter writers," joking that one day she might be better remembered for her correspondence than for her books ("awful vision for you").[1] While that hasn't happened, and doesn't appear likely to happen, it's true that her letters are witty, heartfelt, and a joy to read—and for that matter, so are his.

Given all this, it seems strange that so few are aware of their friendship. When I began to tell friends and acquaintances about my idea for this book, surprise at the very fact that Lewis and Sayers were friends was a common reaction.

And in some ways that's understandable. For one thing, their friendship was shorter than many of Lewis's other, more celebrated ones—only a decade and a half. For another, their public personas today scarcely touch at any point.

Lewis's memory is kept alive largely by the Christian world—through *Mere Christianity*, *The Screwtape Letters*, *The Great Divorce*, and many more—and by the many fans of his Chronicles of Narnia series for children. Sayers is remembered chiefly as the great mystery writer who challenged Agatha Christie for the title of Queen of Crime (and, some of us would argue, beat Christie soundly in that department), and, among many homeschool and classical education enthusiasts, for an essay that she wrote on educational methods.

These are only a couple of many possible reasons that the story of their friendship—or of Sayers's role as a mid-twentieth-century apologist, for that matter—is not all that well known today outside the academic realm. Another possible reason is Sayers's reluctance to evangelize, a reluctance that can be difficult to understand for the evangelicals who treasure Lewis's work for, among other things, his straightforward embrace of that role. There's also the fact that Sayers was a woman—and a woman with a skeleton in her closet, at that—another aspect difficult to reckon with for many modern evangelicals used to following and elevating primarily male leaders, thinkers, and writers. As if that weren't enough, the way she dealt with that skeleton in the closet was decidedly strange, at least for us denizens of the twenty-first century.

And it probably doesn't help matters that Sayers was a woman of fierce independence, with certain of her ideas almost incomprehensible to today's evangelical ways of thinking. Or that her home life was not exactly conventional.

(Neither was Lewis's, for that matter, but sometimes Christian men get away with these things more easily than do Christian women.) Or maybe it's simply that Sayers came to her role as an apologist, and to her friendship with Lewis, relatively late in life, having already become famous as a writer of detective stories.

But Sayers, like Lewis, was also a gifted writer on both religious and academic subjects. They differed on many things—and were not shy about expressing their differences—but at bottom they shared certain fundamental values that bound them together. They could, and did, talk to each other about anything from the possible ordination of women to the difficulties of translating Dante's *Inferno*, sometimes veering into subjects like the raising of hens. And in the process, they gradually helped to shape each other's thinking and writing.

Not that either may have recognized the fact. Lewis called his close friend J. R. R. Tolkien impossible to influence; he probably would have said the same, even more emphatically, of the eccentric woman who fought passionately with him over questions of theology and writing. But as many have demonstrated, it wasn't actually true of Tolkien, and, I would argue, it wasn't true of Sayers either. It's possible that she never would have developed into the skilled Christian apologist she became if not for Lewis's quiet but persistent encouragement. It's certain that she hadn't wanted to.

"Meanwhile, I am left with the Atheist on my hands," she complained to Lewis in a 1943 letter, about a correspondent who kept pestering her about religion. "I do not want him. I have no use for him. I have no missionary zeal at all. God is behaving with His usual outrageous lack of scruple." She had suggested some reading to the man, but not without trepidation.

> If he reads any of the books I have recommended, he will write me long and disorderly letters about them. It will go on for years. I cannot bear it. Two of the books are yours—I only hope they will rouse him to fury. Then I shall hand him on to you. You like souls. I don't. God is simply taking advantage of the fact that I can't stand intellectual chaos, and it isn't fair.[2]

God and Lewis both, perhaps. As loudly as she protested against being drawn into the role of apologist, something kept allowing her to be drawn—quite likely, the influence of the friend who saw in her a gift she didn't see, and didn't even want to see, in herself.

And what of her influence on him? Sayers's mention of a lack of "up-to-date books about Miracles" that she could recommend to the atheist, in that very same letter, is believed by many to have inspired Lewis to write his own book on the subject. But her effect on him went far beyond just giving him book topic suggestions.

Lewis was admittedly, and famously, most comfortable among a circle of male friends. Every element of his upbringing, his era, and his surroundings had shaped him to feel this way. This is another reason many people don't think of Dorothy L. Sayers when they think of Lewis and friendship. The standard story we hear about him was that the Inklings, a group consisting of Lewis himself, his brother, Tolkien, and various other male friends, gave him the help and feedback he needed on his writings before he published them.

This is true, as far as it goes. But there's much more to the story than that. Though no women were part of the Inklings, Lewis had several female friends and correspondents outside that circle, including Anglican nun Sister Penelope Lawson and poet Ruth Pitter, whose judgment and sense he relied on.

Sayers was also one of these women, and as such, she helped to make sure that his world was much broader and deeper and richer than any "men only" world, even the most intelligent and devout one, could ever be. Though she liked and respected Lewis always, some of his writings about the roles and nature of men and women caused her to raise a cynical eyebrow, figuratively speaking. Still, she was patient and diplomatic with him (or as diplomatic as it was possible for her to be), asserting her own ideas on the subject without compromise but also without contempt. And she noticed and appreciated the changes in his thinking on the subject over the years—changes she herself had helped make happen.

It's true that Sayers's connections with Lewis and other members of his circle are known, acknowledged, and studied by scholars. All told, seven of these writers—George MacDonald, G. K. Chesterton, C. S. Lewis, Owen Barfield, J. R. R. Tolkien, Charles Williams, and Dorothy L. Sayers—were woven together in a tight web of influence and affinity that made them absolutely indispensable to each other. These are the writers whose papers and effects are curated at the Marion E. Wade Center at Wheaton College; written about in its journal, *VII*; studied at the C. S. Lewis Summer Institutes; and generally grouped together by those who know them best. As Dr. Barbara Reynolds, Sayers's friend, goddaughter, and biographer, explained in a lecture:

Professor Clyde S. Kilby [founder of the Wade Center], in that brilliant vision which he had of the seven authors who belonged together, was right to include Sayers . . . not just as the token woman but as someone who might, perhaps, be called "an honorary Inkling."[3]

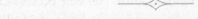

These seven were also the writers featured in a course at Messiah College in the 1990s called Theology and Oxford Christian Writers. At the time I signed up for this course, I knew very little of any of them. I was most familiar with Lewis, but only to a limited extent. Somehow, despite a reasonably well-read childhood, I had managed to miss Narnia completely, but as a teenager I had read and enjoyed *Mere Christianity* and, if I remember correctly, *The Screwtape Letters* as well. *The Hobbit* to me was just some book that my sister had balked at having to read in junior high school and had to be dragged through, protesting all the way, by our mother. The rest were, to the best of my recollection now, a complete blank.

But I was intrigued enough by Lewis that the promise of learning more of him, along with his friends and associates, lured me in. It wasn't just because of the depth, wit, and clarity of his writing, though of course that was a large part of it. The plain truth is, having come from a strict Independent Fundamental Baptist high school that had a six-inch rule between boys and girls and regarded alcohol as little short of poison, I was in a mood to be attracted to a genial Christian apologist who drank wine and smoked cigars and generally took life a lot easier.

But I got even more than I bargained for. It's not an exaggeration to say that what I learned in that class changed my whole life.

In Lewis I found, as I already expected, not just a brilliant storyteller but a wise and appealing guide to faith whose words would sink deeply into my mind, heart, and soul. In many of the other authors, I found additional wisdom, imagination, and wit. And I finally learned to appreciate, even to love, hobbits. But in Sayers, I found a kindred spirit. Her very eccentricities delighted me. Having read one of her sparkling and brilliant mystery novels, *Gaudy Night*, for class, I promptly headed for the campus library to get the rest of them. And after reading her play cycle on the life of Christ, *The Man Born to Be King*, I wanted to read everything else she had to say about faith.

To this day, Sayers and Lewis are two of my three favorite authors (Charles Dickens being the other one). And their warm, acerbic, funny friendship has been a source of endless fascination. Of the web of relationships I learned about in that class, theirs has been one of the most intriguing to me—perhaps because it's one of the least discussed. In a way, you could say I had to find it for myself, digging it out of the respective collections of their letters, piecing it together from one missive to the next, delighting in the little discoveries I made about each of them and their thoughts on each other. As Justin Phillips suggests in his book *C. S. Lewis at the BBC:*

> They lived in an era when the best way to build up and maintain a friendship was by writing a letter. If ever mutual regard was founded on shared respect and nurtured by correspondence, there are few examples as convincing as the friendship between Lewis and Sayers.[4]

That friendship, like any good friendship, brought out aspects of their characters that weren't quite like the aspects brought out by any of their other relationships. As Lewis himself wrote in *The Four Loves*, "In each of my friends there is something that only some other friend can fully bring out."[5] What Lewis and Sayers brought out in each other will be explored in the coming pages. But it's not giving away too much to say here that, despite the differences in views, experiences, and temperament that sometimes caused friction between them, Dorothy Sayers and Jack Lewis "got" each other on a surprisingly deep and intuitive level.

The neglected story of their friendship has much to offer us—far more, I would argue, than just fresh light on the development of their respective careers and worldviews. In any time and place it would resonate, but perhaps especially in our particular cultural moment—a moment when many Christians are questioning the wisdom of cross-gender friendships, and when many of us in general are prone to exist inside "bubbles" filled with others just like us.

It seems that in every generation, we come up with new reasons to restrict friendships between men and women. When Lewis and Sayers were growing up, and even when they were well into adulthood, there was a whole host of reasons given for keeping the worlds of the different genders separate, the most prominent one being that women were seen as being best suited to home and hearth, not academia or the workforce. The utter arbitrariness of some of these restrictions—for instance, the fact that young Dorothy L. Sayers was able to go to college at Oxford University, and even earn first-class honors, but was not given a degree until years later—underscored their foolishness.

Fast-forward about a hundred years, and in our time, developments in both the Christian world and in the wider, secular world have made cross-gender friendships a renewed source of friction. As I write these words, we're facing an absolute epidemic of revelations about sexual harassment, abuse, and assault that leave no sector of society untouched—from the entertainment industry all the way to the local church. Some of our most beloved cultural and religious heroes have proven to be anything but heroic, as victims who kept a stiff upper lip their entire lives finally began to feel free to speak out. There's even such a case in the story I'm about to tell. It involved neither Lewis nor Sayers directly, but it did involve someone to whom both were close—someone they both fervently believed was above suspicion, indeed almost saintly. Even the wisest and most sensible among us are sometimes prone to misjudgment.

Faced with such devastation, we scramble desperately for solutions, or at least stopgaps. As so often happens in a time of crisis, some of the solutions being proposed are drastic—including increasing isolation and segregation of the sexes. Many in the church question the wisdom of men and women who are not married to each other spending any significant time together. Meetings, meals, and drives together are widely seen as unnecessary at best, dangerous at worst. They can lead to temptation, to accusations (both true and false), to all kinds of bad things. Better to avoid these friendships if at all possible.

So intensely do we focus on the minute details of such relationships and the dozens of different ways that men and women can drag each other to ruin that we lose sight of the bigger picture: namely, how terribly reductive a view this is of ourselves and our fellow human beings. And how anti-Christian. As Aimee Byrd reminds us in her book *Why Can't*

We Be Friends?: *Avoidance Is Not Purity*, it was Sigmund Freud, not Jesus Christ, who taught that practically everything about us—our loves, our interactions, our very identities—was rooted in our sexuality. "The church," Byrd writes, "has accepted and semi-sanctified these reductive views: sexuality is good for landing a spouse, but it's a barrier to friendship because men and women can't possibly just enjoy each other's company."[6] Thus, we burden ourselves with rules and restrictions governing every interaction and every opportunity for fellowship.

The Bible tells us to be careful and wise in how we interact with each other; it doesn't tell us to avoid each other. It took the secular world and its skewed, flawed views to scare us into doing that. In fact, as Byrd points out, some of the greatest friendships in the history of the church—friendships that we can still benefit and learn from today—were cross-gender friendships: St. Teresa of Avila and Father Gerome Gracian, John Calvin and Renée of France, Hannah More and William Wilberforce. These friendships are just a few of the many she could have named. They were not just good for the people who participated in them but were also fruitful, helping those friends to make great contributions to the church and to society.

And that makes perfect sense, because if men and women are different, as the church teaches us, it stands to reason that we need each other to help get us out of our own heads, broaden our perspectives, and increase our understanding and our empathy. This was certainly true of C. S. Lewis and Dorothy L. Sayers. Both were brilliant, well-educated, thoughtful, opinionated Christians. Their views were well-informed and well-thought-out. Yet with all that, each of them still needed something more—a way to look at the world sometimes from another perspective, something or someone to push back against and at the same time offer a new way of looking at things. They found this in each other. Though each of them was a person with many good friends, the unique qualities of each—including their different sexes—gave to the other something that made them stronger, wiser, and better.

This is one of the greatest reasons why the story of their friendship is so valuable. It shows how we can learn to transcend our differences, comprehend our own blind spots, and understand the true value and worth of a friend.

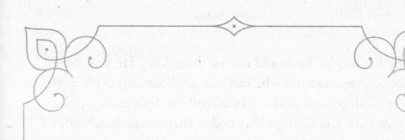

One

"No Mean City"

Oxford and World War I

During the First World War, Oxford—both the university and the town surrounding it—was in turmoil, like the rest of Great Britain. Both students and citizens were rapidly enlisting, and college buildings were being used for training, as hospitals, and to house refugees from the war-torn European continent.[1] The change was, to say the least, disconcerting, not just for those who knew the once-peaceful university town well but even for those who were new to it. "The effect of the war here is much more startling than I could have expected, and everything is very homely and out of order," wrote Clive Staples "Jack" Lewis to his father, Albert Lewis, two days after his arrival at Oxford University on April 26, 1917.[2]

Eighteen-year-old Jack had long dreamed of attending the university. But when he arrived that spring, it was with the knowledge he would not be there long. He was there for academic reasons—he had won a scholarship to University College, one of the several colleges that make up the university, and he began his studies there immediately after arriving—but also for military reasons. He was to join the Officers' Training Corps just four days after his arrival, and by October he would be in the army.

Meanwhile, twenty-three-year-old Dorothy Leigh Sayers had arrived in Oxford the very day after Lewis had. The same April Saturday that found Jack writing to his father found Dorothy writing to her parents as well, to tell them about her new living arrangements at 17 Long Wall Street: "The staircase window looks upon New College Chapel, and the garden is tucked in under the Old Walls, so I am rather jollily placed as far as Oxford goes."[3]

The Life of the Mind

At this point, Dorothy and Jack were living less than half a mile from each other. Yet they were at opposite ends of their college careers. Dorothy had finished her studies in modern languages in 1915, at Somerville College, achieving first-class honors in French.

However, Jack would still receive the first of his degrees before Dorothy received hers. Oxford University, as I mentioned earlier, did not grant degrees to women when Dorothy was going to college. They only changed their policy in 1920; when they did, Dorothy was in the first group of women to receive them.

After graduation, Dorothy had tried teaching for a while but didn't like it. Attempts to train as a nurse didn't work out either. Restless and searching for a truly satisfying job, she had come back to Oxford in this spring of 1917 to work as an apprentice to publisher Basil Blackwell, who was then running his family's publishing and bookselling business there. That business happened to have already published Dorothy's first book, a volume of poems titled simply *Op. 1*, in 1916. It was part of a series of books by young poets titled Adventurers All, which, as we will see, could not have been more appropriate for this particular young poet.

It made perfect sense that Dorothy would return to Oxford. Even though she found the idea of an academic career stifling and boring, she nonetheless loved the place with a passion. All her life she was proud of having been born in the university town, where her father, the Rev. Henry Sayers, had been headmaster of the Cathedral Choir School. "I am a citizen of no mean city" was the beginning of the first sentence of her unfinished memoir, *My Edwardian Childhood*, applying Paul's words about Tarsus in Acts 21:39 to her own illustrious birthplace.[4] She used the quote again in *Gaudy Night*, considered by many her greatest novel (largely set at the university), and went on to add: "It might be an old and an old-fashioned city, with inconvenient buildings and narrow streets where the passers-by squabbled foolishly about the right of way; but her foundations were set upon the holy hills and her spires touched heaven."[5]

At the age of four, Dorothy had moved with her family from Oxford to Bluntisham, a small country parish where her father was to become the new rector. But in some ways she never stopped considering herself a citizen of Oxford. The beauty and the stateliness of the place stayed with her, and something more: the love of learning that the university represented to her. Even though she was not destined for an academic career, the life of the mind, and the habits of thinking that went with it, would be a crucial part of her life. In *Gaudy Night*, again, she puts these words in the mouth of Lord Peter Wimsey when he comes back to visit Oxford, weary and discouraged after weeks of dealing with international politics (no easy task in mid-1930s Europe, for obvious reasons):

> Here's where the real things are done . . . if only those bun-glers out there will keep quiet and let it go on. God! How I loathe haste and violence and all that ghastly, slippery clever-ness. Unsound, unscholarly, unsincere—nothing but propa-ganda and special pleading and "what do we get out of this?" No time, no peace, no silence; nothing but conferences and newspapers and public speeches till one can't hear oneself think. . . . If only one could root one's self in here among the grass and stones and do something worth doing, even if it was only restoring a lost breathing for the love of the job and nothing else.[6]

Both Peter Wimsey and Harriet Vane, the novel's heroine, would leave the university again after a time of spiritual, mental, and emotional renewal to go back to life in the out-side world—much as Dorothy L. Sayers herself did. Despite the insincerity and superficiality of that outside world, these two characters, like their creator, recognized it as the place where their callings and their responsibilities lay. But like them, Dorothy would consider Oxford a touchstone, a place where truth was honored and pursued and where values that had been forgotten might be restored.

A Writer or a Scholar

As for young Jack Lewis, it was never a question that he was destined for an academic career. His gifts, interests, and capabilities—and lack thereof, such as his great difficulty in working with his hands—were such that it was doubtful whether he would be fit for any other kind of work. "You may make a writer or a scholar of him, but you'll not make anything else," Lewis later recalled his beloved tutor, William T. Kirkpatrick, telling his father.[7] Jack himself wholeheartedly agreed with this assessment.

Jack Lewis and his older brother, Warren, having lost their mother at a young age, had grown up near Belfast, Ireland, with their father. Both boys had a difficult relationship with Albert Lewis, finding him hard to talk to and constantly feeling that he misunderstood them. Along with his close relationship with his brother, young Jack depended heavily on his fertile imagination and the books, music, and natural scenery he loved to sustain him.

As he grew up, the prospect of higher education and the prospect of the military—as widely different as they were, and as much as he preferred the former to the latter— combined to offer a way out. As biographer George Sayer explains:

> Jack could have avoided military service if he had gone to an Irish university, but no Irish university had the glamour of Oxford, and worse, going to one might mean he would have to live at home. Perhaps, too, Warren's patriotism [his brother had joined the army in 1914] had some influence on him.[8]

As it turned out, it was his military service that would ensure Jack's entrance to Oxford, for though he had been able to gain a scholarship to the university, he could not pass the mathematics portion of the actual entrance exam that every prospective student was required to take. He was forced to depend on the waiver that Oxford offered to those who served in the war. Given that he would go on to take not one but three firsts—a first being the highest academic honor one could achieve—it's staggering to think that a lack of ability in math could have kept this brilliant young man out of the university altogether. (Especially when one considers that Jack's mother, Flora, had been gifted in mathematics! Apparently that was one gene that had failed to get passed down.)

Fortunately, skills in mathematics were not needed for the position that Jack would attain after earning his final degree: a fellowship at Magdalen College, Oxford, where he would teach English and philosophy. He would hold that position for the next twenty-nine years. It's no wonder that, to this day, Oxford is so closely associated with Lewis, and with his circle of friends, that his fans come in droves to visit the university, and organizations such as the C. S. Lewis Institute hold conferences there to study and discuss his life, faith, and work.

Though Oxford was at the center of his life for so long, Jack's attitude toward the place was not quite the rapturous one Dorothy would display all her life. It would be a mistake to think that he knew the place itself better than she did, after her long history with it. But it may be that her subsequent distance from it helped to keep it fresh and lovable in her memory. Lewis knew something of the workaday atmosphere for a teacher there, as Sayers did not (and, it will be recalled, as she didn't wish to). More specifically, he would eventually come to know what it was like to be a Christian apologist there.

What we sometimes forget, when we think of C. S. Lewis and Oxford as being tied so closely together, is that Oxford University in the twentieth century was not exactly the ideal place for a popular teacher and writer on the Christian faith. In that rarefied academic atmosphere, popular success was looked on with a touch of suspicion—and when that success was tied to Christianity, suspicion tended to deepen into outright alarm. Despite his fondness for his work and for the university, his exemplary service there was not always rewarded as it should have been, and at times he had good reason to feel hurt and even betrayed.

But in 1917, at the beginning of his college career, these aspects of the future could not have been further from young Jack Lewis's mind. He was eager to begin his studies and determined to find success—and, as we will see, during this period of his life the Christian faith played no part in his vision of his future.

And in fairness to Dorothy, it would be wrong to give the impression that she thought of Oxford as perfect. As a woman, she knew a little bit about what discrimination at Oxford was like, as *Gaudy Night*—even while it spent so much time paying glowing tribute to the place—would make clear. So in her own way, she could relate to some of what Jack went through there.

The Shadow of War

In 1917, Sayers and Lewis were at opposite ends of their wartime experience as well as their educational one. At this point, Lewis was about to begin his service in the "War to End All Wars." After completing his training and receiving his commission as an officer, he would arrive at the front in France on November 29 of that year, his nineteenth birthday.

By his own account, his very first reaction to the fighting was—typical for Lewis—an intellectual and literary one. In *Surprised by Joy: The Shape of My Early Life*, he would write:

> One imaginative moment seems now to matter more than the realities that followed. It was the first bullet I heard—so far from me that it "whined" like a journalist's or a peacetime poet's bullet. At that moment there was something not exactly like fear, much less like indifference: a little quavering signal that said, "This is War. This is what Homer wrote about."[9]

Lewis would serve in the war until April 1918, when he was wounded and two other men in his unit were killed by friendly fire—a British shell landed among them. He spent several months recovering and was officially demobilized in December 1918.

The war for Lewis, as for so many others, was a nightmarish experience that would haunt his mind and imagination. Throughout his life, it would make itself felt in his writing. In *A Hobbit, a Wardrobe, and a Great War*, Joseph Loconte traces themes and descriptions inspired by the war throughout Lewis's work, as well as J. R. R. Tolkien's. Peter's battle with the Wolf in *The Lion, the Witch and the Wardrobe*, described in rather gruesome detail for a children's story ("He was tugging and pulling and the Wolf seemed neither alive nor dead . . ."), is just one of many examples.[10]

"Lewis once admitted that his memories of war invaded his dreams for years," Loconte writes. "His account of Peter's battle could have been any soldier's recollection of bayoneting the enemy for the first time."[11]

But the war affected Lewis's thinking in far deeper ways than just helping him to understand the classical poets better or providing vivid images to incorporate into his fiction. Like many writers who served in that war, he emerged with his worldview altered—but not necessarily in ways that those familiar with the post–World War I generation of writers might expect. That generation as a rule displayed a marked bitterness and cynicism in their writing, having experienced the death of illusion and hope in the mud-filled trenches. They felt they had been sent to "die as cattle," as Wilfred Owen, one of the greatest of the World War I poets, wrote in "Anthem for Doomed Youth"—and for no good reason.[12] Their anger, resentment, and pain burned unmistakably and unforgettably in their words.

If this was the case for those who had once been high-spirited and hopeful young men, then certainly Jack Lewis, who had already felt himself to be thoroughly disillusioned and pessimistic before the war, might have come out of his war experience with those qualities hardened into permanence. Strangely, just the opposite seems to have happened. Not that he was now ready to give up his pessimism completely, but the foundation of it, far from hardening, was beginning to crack just a little. As Joseph Loconte puts it, "The sorrows of war did not ultimately blacken Lewis's creative life."[13]

Loconte suggests that part of the reason for this was that Lewis's personal wartime experience offered a study in contrasts that had caught his attention and left a deep impression. There had been great horror, pain, and grief, and yet—when Lewis was sent to the hospital in London after being wounded—there had also been unexpected beauty.

> It seems likely that the simple pleasure of a train ride through the English countryside, set against the dreariness and horror of war, created for Lewis a powerful experience of joy: a sensation so compelling that it undermined his materialist outlook. . . . The experience appears to have wrought a change in Lewis—a small change, perhaps, but a permanent one. It quickened his belief in a spiritual, other-worldly source of natural beauty.[14]

As fans of Lewis will recognize, Loconte does not use the word *joy* lightly or accidentally; it was the word that to Lewis represented an emotional and spiritual experience powerful enough to impact, even to change, one's whole life. Since childhood, experiences of joy—beginning with the simple but never-forgotten moment when he had first seen a perfect toy garden fashioned by his brother from moss, flowers, twigs, and leaves—had been the defining moments of his life.

For one as impressionable and sensitive as Lewis had always been, the return to a beautiful place after those months of squalor and terror could not help but leave an indelible mark.

In the Middle of Things

Meanwhile, things had been decidedly different for Dorothy L. Sayers regarding the war. Back in the fateful summer of 1914, she and two friends had actually gone off to war-threatened France for a vacation. They were, as Sayers's biographer Barbara Reynolds remarked with wry understatement, "strangely unaware of the gravity of the international situation."[15]

But perhaps it wasn't actually as strange as it might seem. For a girl both sheltered and spirited, a girl who had once spent much of her time dressing up as Athos from *The Three Musketeers* and pressing family and friends into performing various other roles in the story—who, in short, saw life as an amusing adventure—her activities that summer could hardly be called out of character.[16] Like Lewis, she was inclined to see things through a literary lens; unlike him, she may have been able to let that lens, at least at this time in her life, distance her a little too far from reality.

Even when that reality finally forced itself upon her and her friends, irrepressible Dorothy reported back to her family that being "right in the middle of things" in a rapidly mobilizing country was "frightfully exciting," comparing it to something out of a book by fantasy and science fiction writer H. G. Wells.[17] For all that, she eventually had to leave the excitement behind her to return to her schooling. But back in Oxford, she still found time, at least for a while, to help some of the many Belgian refugees who had fled there.

And as insouciant as she may have seemed about it all at the time, the shadow of the war fell on her own life and work as well. The famous fictional detective she would create, Lord Peter Wimsey, strode upon the scene with a manner equally insouciant, bordering on flippant. Yet his war-induced shell shock—what we would call PTSD today—would play a significant role in more than one of the books in the Wimsey series. As Peter's mother observes with characteristic understatement in the first book, *Whose Body?*, after Peter experiences a sudden and unexpected attack of the malady for the first time in several years, "Nerves are such funny things . . . and I suppose we can't expect to forget all about a great war in a year or two."[18]

In some ways, though she couldn't have known it then, Sayers was foreshadowing her own future experiences with a husband who would suffer lifelong, steadily worsening effects of his war service. Indeed, it would take much longer than a year or two for the great war to fade into the past. Both Lewis and Sayers were fortunate to be among those equipped with enough natural resilience to get through the aftermath and to help others through it. Still, like the rest of their generation, they could not help but carry the marks of it with them throughout their lives.

Faith Confirmed, Faith Lost

On the surface, C. S. Lewis and Dorothy L. Sayers were in very different places in 1917, religiously speaking. Raised as an Anglican, Jack had lost his faith at the age of fifteen. In *Surprised by Joy*, he would cite a number of different factors that led to his deconversion, not all of which seem like compatible factors. A beloved and admired teacher's interest in occultism, difficulties in his prayer life, struggles with lust and masturbation, the previously mentioned pessimistic bent to his nature that led him to see the universe as "a menacing and unfriendly place"—each of these played a role. "I do not think I achieved any logical connection between [occultism and atheism]," he wrote, trying to explain how both of these widely divergent strains of thought could have been influencing him at the same time. "They swayed me in different moods, and had only this in common, that both made against Christianity."[19]

This was a notable early example of what was to be a common theme of Lewis's life: the relationship between the rational intellect and the romantic imagination. The effort to resolve the struggle between them would serve as a significant factor in his return to faith many years later. He simply could not find a way to satisfy the claims of both and still remain an atheist; his imagination insisted on hungering for things that his intellect told him could not be true if God did not exist. As biographer Alan Jacobs put it, "He went through a period of years where he did everything he could to kill that part of him that was drawn to the symbols, the images, the myths—the beauty of art. Ultimately, he couldn't kill it."[20]

In later life Lewis would develop an ability to harmonize the two strains of thought in what would become one of the most attractive and memorable features of his writing. But for now, according to his own account, he was content to take what he believed he needed from each strain without attempting to bring them into accord with each other.

One of the great regrets of Lewis's life was that, despite his loss of belief, he had agreed to be confirmed in the Anglican church as a teenager to please his father. Years later, he would go so far as to call it "one of the worst acts of my life."[21] By the time he wrote those words, he had come back to the faith, and had come to understand what a grave sin it was to be confirmed and take communion without believing in Christ. Even at the time the event took place, he was aware he was being hypocritical by participating in a ceremony that meant absolutely nothing to him. But at that time, all he cared about was going along with what his father wanted and thus avoiding a scene.

Jack Lewis was not the only one with miserable memories of being confirmed; surprisingly, Dorothy L. Sayers also had a few of her own. This despite the fact that, unlike Lewis, she never deliberately gave up her Christian faith. For Dorothy, the reasons for regret were different and more complicated. In fact—unusually for her—she hardly seems to have known her own mind on the subject. In her biography of Sayers, Barbara Reynolds attempts to navigate the inconsistent statements about her confirmation that Sayers made over the years, in order to try to decipher her true thoughts and feelings.

At seventeen, Dorothy wrote to her parents from boarding school, apparently without any misgivings at all, that she was "to be confirmed this year" with the rest of her class.[22] Although she was a clergyman's daughter, Henry and Helen Sayers had never put the kind of pressure on Dorothy that Albert Lewis put on Jack, and Reynolds opines that "it is unlikely that Dorothy's parents would have given instruction for her to be confirmed . . . without consulting her."[23] After the event, she wrote to tell them that it had been "an awfully nice service . . . most beautifully arranged." She gives them a detailed description of it all, but adds at the end: "I never can write about my *feelings*—that's why I haven't."[24]

As Reynolds points out, this is a wildly uncharacteristic statement, since Dorothy was normally quite happy to write to her parents about her feelings on all sorts of other matters, from fashion to schoolwork to the theater, often (at this time in her life) with a plethora of adjectives and exclamation points. Something was going on here, as Dorothy herself made clear in another letter, this one written twenty years later to her cousin Ivy Shrimpton, when they were discussing the possible baptism of Dorothy's son.

> Being baptised against one's will is not nearly so harmful as being confirmed against one's will, which is what happened to me and gave me a resentment against religion which lasted a long time. My people (weakly) thought it would "be better" to have it "done" at school—and it was the worst possible school for the purpose, being Low Church and sentimental—and I (still more weakly) gave in because I didn't want to be conspicuous and fight it out. Afterwards, when I became High Church, I wished I hadn't done it, because then I could have undertaken it properly, without fury and resentment, and without having the dreariest associations connected with the Communion Service.[25]

Her words here are so completely different from her earlier words on the matter that they require some unpacking. It's certainly possible that, twenty years later, she could no longer remember exactly how she had felt or what she had said about her confirmation at the time. But the strength of her feelings expressed in the letter to Ivy Shrimpton make that unlikely. It's much likelier she had hidden what she really thought from her parents, wanting to spare their feelings and make things easy for them—or she was torn over the whole affair.

Sayers appears to have left a significant clue, though, in *Cat o'Mary*, an autobiographical novel she began writing in the mid-1930s but never completed. In this story, she has her young protagonist, Katherine, write to her parents almost exactly the same thing that young Dorothy had written to hers: "I won't say anything about *feelings*. . . . I can't express those very well."[26] Although it's generally unwise to identify an author too closely with one of her characters,[27] the similarity of the passages here (especially with a novel that was intended to be autobiographical) indicates that Katherine's "feelings" on the matter are much the same as Dorothy's had been.

And what Katherine feels is that the version of Christianity she has been taught all her life places entirely too *much* emphasis on feelings and too little emphasis on what mattered most to her: intellect and imagination. Christianity, in Katherine's (and Dorothy's) experience, is something referred to in hushed and overreverent whispers, almost as if there were something indecent about it. There's nothing robust about it, nothing she can sink her teeth into. Quite the contrary—in her reluctant preparations for her confirmation, Katherine is overwhelmed by "the sense of butting against something soft and stuffy."[28]

For anyone acquainted with Dorothy's writing, her revulsion at this sort of overly sentimental and exaggeratedly pious religious rhetoric and practice rings true. All her life, she would be completely put off by any hint of religious sentimentality. The Christian faith, to her, was something strong and splendid and above all intellectual, something that spoke to her mind before her heart. The emotions that for so many are attendant on Christianity were like a foreign language to her; the doctrine of Christianity was something her mind could wrestle with and emerge satisfied and refreshed. (Just a glance at the titles of some of the religious essays she would write later in life reveals this proclivity: "Strong Meat," "The Dogma Is the Drama," and "Creed or Chaos?" for example.) Any attempt to make Christianity cloying or treacly or sentimental nauseated her, and, more importantly, seemed to her to dishonor God and diminish the faith.

It is difficult, though, to understand exactly what she meant when she wrote of her subsequent "resentment" of religion. After her confirmation she continued, at least outwardly, to practice her religion faithfully and to attend church. And her letters continued to show an active interest in the subject. She told her mother—apparently without fear of disapproval—that even though she believed, she still felt the need to work things out for herself in that area. This in her case was not a sign of individualism or of a desire to be "spiritual but not religious"—that was the very last thing Sayers ever would have wanted to be. The very term reeks of the pleasant, feel-good vagueness that always repelled her when it came to religion. She simply had a great need to learn and to understand more about what exactly she was subscribing to.

A Shared Guide

It was around this time that Dorothy began to develop a great attachment to the works of the popular Catholic writer G. K. Chesterton, who wrote of the Christian faith as something splendid, shining, and true. She knew and liked Chesterton's writing before she even knew that he was a Christian, but, as she wrote to her parents, she was not surprised to learn that he was one—"a very cheerful one."[29] Not only was he cheerful, but he also wrote things like this about the Christian faith: "In my vision the heavenly chariot flies thundering through the ages, the dull heresies sprawling and prostrate, the wild truth reeling but erect."[30]

It was exactly the sort of language to win over a girl who had once swashbuckled around the house dressed as a Musketeer. In fact, the whole combination of cheerfulness, exciting imagery, and firm doctrine was a tonic for her. There was nothing pleasantly vague about Chesterton's personality or his writing in the least, and no suggestion in his work that Christianity had anything dull, tedious, or sappy about it. So exactly were his work and personality suited to her temperament, and so much did she learn from him, that Dorothy would one day write to his widow, Frances: "I think, in some ways, G. K.'s books have become more a part of my mental makeup than those of any writer you could name."[31]

This attachment to Chesterton was, in fact, an attachment she and Jack Lewis would soon have in common—despite the latter's complete lack of faith during these years. Lewis first read some of Chesterton's essays while recuperating from his war wound in 1918. Of course, it was hardly the first time Lewis had encountered a Christian author, and it wasn't even the first time such an encounter had been life-altering. As most Lewis fans know, his experience reading George MacDonald's *Phantastes* shortly before the war would be a transformative one, by which his "imagination was, in a certain sense, baptized."[32]

But that had been a different type of reading experience. Though Lewis was aware of MacDonald's Christianity, it was implicit in a fantasy novel, Lewis's favorite genre during his adolescence and young adulthood. He could savor the story without embracing MacDonald's ideas about faith (or so he thought at the time!). Chesterton, on the other hand, was writing essays, a much more direct form of communication, and in them was quite open about his Christianity.

Yet somehow it didn't turn off the young Lewis—quite the opposite. Joseph Pearce, who has written extensively on both Lewis and Chesterton, writes of the former's reading of the latter:

> In spite of the fact that Lewis was an atheist at the time, he couldn't help liking Chesterton's jollity, his sense of humour, and his rumbustious *joie de vivre*. Chesterton had more common sense than all the moderns put together, the young atheist believed, except of course for his Christianity.[33]

Rumbustious may be an unusual word, but it's the perfect word to describe G. K. Chesterton, and—somewhat surprisingly, given their very different personalities at this time—it was the quality in him that appealed to both Jack Lewis and Dorothy Sayers. There's something in the word that signifies "cheerful" common sense, boisterous glee, and a sense of grandeur, all at the same time. It's a quality that morbid introspection simply cannot stand up against. So Chesterton's writing was a tonic that acted on each according to his or her nature. While he was solidifying and shoring up Dorothy's faith, he was helping to clear some of the cobwebs out of Jack's mind. Both still had a long spiritual path to walk, in their differing ways, but they were now sharing a guide.

Tales and Spirits

Not that they were aware of it at the time, of course. Although they lived closer to each other in those months in 1917 than they ever would again, Dorothy Sayers and Jack Lewis did not yet meet, as far as anyone knows. Their later letters to each other give no sign of a previous acquaintance. Did the ebullient young working woman and the intense young university student ever even cross paths during those months? If they did, we have no way of knowing. Nor can we know what they would have thought of each other if they had, though it's fun to speculate.

If they had run across each other, say, at Blackwell's Book-shop—as an Oxford University student and an assistant in the publishing side of Blackwell's business might very well have done—it's quite possible that they would have thought little of each other at this point in their lives. It's true that both were brilliant scholars and talented writers, even when young—that much they had in common, and it's possible that it could have formed the basis of a friendship. However, based on what we know of them at this time via their letters and other writings, it seems likely that Dorothy might have been impatient with, even repelled by, Jack's views and his reserved personality. She had little liking for gloom and introspection, and no tolerance at all for anyone she suspected of being a poseur, and one suspects that some of Jack's more morbid ideas and moods might have given her that impression of him. He, meanwhile, probably would have had no idea what to make of her high spirits and—despite her inward uncertainties—her sometimes belligerent convictions. Perhaps it's downright providential, then, that their first meeting did not take place until much later.

It's an interesting exercise, and a helpful guide to the state of mind of each of our subjects in their early adulthood, to look at the poems they were producing during these years. Like Sayers, who as noted became a published poet in 1916, Lewis also gravitated toward poetry. In fact, each of them would publish a book of poems in 1919, a couple of years after they had lived so near to each other at Oxford. Lewis published his first volume, *Spirits in Bondage*, in March of that year, six months before Sayers released her second volume, *Catholic Tales and Christian Songs*.[34]

The title of that book alone clearly indicated that, despite all Sayers's doubts and difficulties with Christianity, it had nonetheless established a firm grip on her mind and spirit. And the contents of the book more than lived up to the title. *Catholic Tales and Christian Songs** opens with a ballad that reflects all the enthusiasms and passions of Dorothy's young life—and ties Christ firmly to them. He is pictured as both "a bonny outlaw" and "a prince of fairy-tale," a ragged but gallant figure calling to a lady (the poet herself?) to follow him "through the wet and windy weather." The poem ends with these lines from His mouth:

> Here be dragons to be slain, here be rich rewards to
> gain . . .
> If we perish in the seeking, . . . why, how small a
> thing is death![35]

---

*A word about Sayers's use of the term *catholic*: as a high church Anglican—a member of a church that positions itself as the "middle way" between Catholicism and Protestantism—she considered herself more Catholic than Protestant. The term "Anglo-Catholic" is used frequently in her writings to describe her beliefs. Interestingly, in her essay "Dante and Milton," she would write, "I can be at home in the universe of Dante's mind as I cannot be in Milton's, because Dante and I share the same faith," identifying with Dante's Catholicism rather than Milton's Protestantism. See "Dante and Milton," originally written in 1952 for the Summer School of Italian Studies, in Sayers, *Further Papers on Dante, Volume 2: His Heirs and His Ancestors* (Eugene, OR: Wipf & Stock, 2006), 151. See also Kathryn Wehr's excellent and helpful article "Disambiguation: Sayers as a Catholic," *VII: Journal of the Marion E. Wade Center*, vol. 33 (2016): 7–17, which explains how Sayers consistently grouped together Anglicanism, Roman Catholicism, and Orthodoxy under the heading of "Catholic."

This was the Christ whom Dorothy L. Sayers sought, hoped for, and believed in despite everything: a figure both courageous and merry, bent on adventure, battling numerous foes but bound to triumph. The title of the poem, "Desdichado," is taken from Sir Walter Scott's *Ivanhoe*, in which it is the pseudonym used by the eponymous knight before he reveals his true identity. The word as used in the book means "Disinherited One."[36] There was nothing soft or stuffy about this Christ; He scorned the easy, comfortable way, taking the reckless road through life, content to be a "disinherited one" in this world.

The poems in this book demonstrate that although she was still figuring things out, spiritually speaking, young Dorothy Sayers was far ahead of young Jack Lewis when it came to blending the romantic imagination with the rational intellect and expressing the result in literary form. If Jack had been able to see Christ as she did, through the lens of imagination and aspiration rather than classed with everything he feared and hated, he might have been drawn to Him far earlier. But his frame of mind during these years—and the poetry it led him to write—were very different.

As in Dorothy's book, we need not read very far in Jack's book to find a poem that gives a clear and vivid picture of where he was in his spiritual life. After a short poetic prologue, the book's first poem is "Satan Speaks."

Despite the obvious thematic similarities, "Satan Speaks" is no *Screwtape Letters*. The Lewis of these years was unable to achieve the spiritual and philosophical distance from his devilish narrator that would allow him to portray the devil in a realistic way, with all his strengths and his ultimately fatal weaknesses. Rather, the pessimistic young poet identified the devil with the natural world, seeing a "malevolent" force (as he wrote to his friend Arthur Greeves) behind all that exists. It seems that the shift that had begun in him at the end of his war service was still working beneath the surface, not yet having fully freed him from his jaded outlook.

Thus, the poem begins:

> I am Nature, the Mighty Mother,
> I am the law: ye have none other.

The poem goes on to incorporate many of Lewis's war experiences ("I am the battle's filth and strain. . . . I am the bomb, the falling death"). And it goes beyond those horrific memories to the poet's underlying and longstanding belief about the world:

> I am the fact and the crushing reason
> To thwart your fantasy's newborn treason.[37]

Lewis reiterated the difficulty of believing that there was any point to indulging in the world of fancy that he loved, since it apparently could not be reconciled with the brutal and all-consuming world of fact. It's somewhat ironic that he was doing so in a collection of poetry, an art form that could hardly be said to be unfanciful—and, in fact, many of the other poems in the book demonstrated that he still enjoyed and excelled at using his imagination. In the years ahead, it was one of the key forces that would lead to a seismic shift in his worldview.

As things now stood, Dorothy Sayers and Jack Lewis were miles apart in their thinking. But a great deal would change before they first made contact, a full twenty-five years after they had lived so near each other in Oxford.

Two

"A High Wind"

The Beginning of Friendship

It started with a fan letter. That was how C. S. Lewis would remember it, many years later:

> Dorothy Sayers . . . was the first person of importance who ever wrote me a fan-letter. I liked her, originally, because she liked me; later, for the extraordinary zest and edge of her conversation—as I like a high wind.[1]

Dorothy sent the letter to which he referred sometime in 1942—"around the beginning of April," according to Jack's friend, assistant, and biographer Walter Hooper.[2] Once again, at this moment Jack Lewis and Dorothy Sayers could be said to be at opposite ends of their career trajectories.

Dorothy was now the writer of the bestselling Lord Peter Wimsey series of detective novels, written over a period of fourteen years (1923 to 1937), widely ranked with those of

Agatha Christie and other top Golden Age mystery writers. She had also published a "war-time essay" in book form, *Begin Here* (1940), and a groundbreaking book on creativity and theology, *The Mind of the Maker* (1941). Most recently, she had become a successful playwright. The last completed installment of her Lord Peter Wimsey series, *Busman's Honeymoon*, premiered as a play (cowritten with Muriel St. Clare Byrne) in 1936 before it was turned into a novel in 1937.* She had subsequently written more plays, both religious and secular.

In 1941, a play that Dorothy had written about the birth of Christ had caught the eye and ear of James Welch, director of religious programming at the BBC.[3] Welch had commissioned her to write a radio play cycle on the life of Christ, *The Man Born to Be King*, which began airing in weekly installments in December 1941. The plays were a hit—not at all hindered (in fact, probably helped) by the controversy of her insistence on using modern language, including American slang, to tell Christ's story.[4]

At the time she first wrote to Jack, these plays were still airing weekly on the radio. And Dorothy's translation of Dante's *Divine Comedy*—her favorite project and the admitted obsession of her last years—was still ahead of her. But by this time she had already done the vast majority of the work for which she would be best remembered.

Jack, on the other hand, was just now achieving fame as a writer. His main focus was his teaching career at Oxford,

---

*In 1936, Dorothy began work on another Lord Peter novel, to be titled *Thrones, Dominations*, but eventually abandoned it. Long after Dorothy's death, fellow mystery novelist Jill Paton Walsh completed the book, based on the notes that she had left, and published it in 1998.

but he too had found time to publish a few works in quite a wide variety of genres: more poetry (*Dymer* and *The Pilgrim's Regress*), an academic work (*The Allegory of Love*), collections of essays (*The Personal Heresy*, coauthored with E. M. W. Tillyard, and *Rehabilitations*), science fiction (*Out of the Silent Planet*), and a popular work of theology (*The Problem of Pain*).

The early 1940s were a particularly eventful time for Jack. In August 1941, he had begun giving a series of "Broadcast Talks" on the BBC, explaining the basics of Christianity to an ostensibly Christian nation that nonetheless seemed to have forgotten them. Like Sayers's *The Man Born to Be King*, the talks were commissioned by James Welch.

George M. Marsden writes that Welch "estimated that two-thirds of BBC listeners lived without any reference to God. One survey of British army recruits revealed that only 23 percent knew the meaning of Easter."[5] It was *The Problem of Pain* that inspired Welch to ask Jack to speak on the radio, but the moment was particularly appropriate; both he and Jack correctly guessed that a nation in the grip of war would be primed and ready to become reacquainted with the religion it had been letting slide.

Though Jack had no previous experience speaking on the radio, his experience as a teacher helped him with both the writing and the delivery of his talks. They proved so popular that he was subsequently invited to give talks on similar subjects to the troops at various military bases around the country. (The material from these broadcast talks would eventually be developed into the book *Mere Christianity*.)

Popular as the talks were, they were not the only reason C. S. Lewis was rapidly becoming a household name in Great Britain. Also in 1941, he had published *The Screwtape*

Letters, a demon's-eye view of the spiritual life of one ordinary young man, to great acclaim. The conceit of the book, which required the author to look at everything from the devil's point of view, was a difficult one to execute, and, according to Lewis, mentally and spiritually exhausting to maintain. But the effort paid off in a book that, precisely because of its unique perspective, satirical tone, and piercing insights, was destined to become one of the great Christian classics.

The letters had been published one by one in the religious publication *The Guardian* before coming out in book form in February 1942, and as George Sayer writes:

> The letters were an immediate success. Many people who had never heard of *The Guardian* before sought it out just for the letters. . . . The first edition of 2,000 copies [of the book] sold out before publication, and it was reprinted eight times by the end of the year.[6]

The book was also successful in the United States, elevating Jack to worldwide fame.

The Most Reluctant Convert

But wait a minute—what happened to the militant young atheist we left at the close of the last chapter? Clearly, we need to backtrack a little and observe that at this point—as that list of his works and activities makes abundantly clear— C. S. Lewis and Dorothy Sayers were no longer poles apart spiritually.

The story of Lewis's gradual conversion in his thirties, first to theism and then to full-blown belief in the Christian God, is familiar to many of us now. To Lewis himself, of course, it had come as something of a shock. There had been absolutely no room in his plans for the advent of Christian beliefs, let alone Christian writing.

Yet, as he would later recount in his spiritual autobiography, *Surprised by Joy*, he had been steadily and irresistibly drawn to faith over a period of years. Time and again, through reading and through friendship, he had encountered Christians who shook his atheistic convictions. As he had with Chesterton, he would catch himself thinking that this or that person would be wonderful if it just weren't for their Christianity!

But more and more, it began to seem that Christianity was, in fact, an essential part of the person's makeup—perhaps even the very thing that Jack liked so much about the person. Everything in his life and his career—the books he read, the people he met, the subjects he taught—seemed to be conspiring to pull him toward the God he "earnestly desired not to meet."[7] Even when he finally capitulated enough to become a theist, he still strenuously resisted becoming a Christian for two more years.

As so often happened in Jack Lewis's life, it was friendship that helped to make the difference. He had become friends with colleagues J. R. R. Tolkien and Hugo Dyson, both committed Christians: Tolkien a Roman Catholic, Dyson an Anglican. For all of them, friendship entailed long, passionate, argumentative conversations about all the things that mattered most: literature, philosophy, religion. Jack became a member of a group founded by Tolkien, the Kolbitars, "devoted to intensive study of Old Norse literature"—a group that was a sort of precursor to what would be a much more famous group called the Inklings, which would include several of the same members.[8] (That group, which would have the much broader purposes of letting its members read their own works to each other and, sometimes, simply enjoy drinks and conversation together, would not get under way until about the mid-1930s.)

It was a late-night conversation in September 1931 with Tolkien and Dyson that finally tipped the scale for Jack in regard to faith. The conversation had turned to mythology, which Jack loved but referred to as lies. Tolkien corrected him: myths were not lies at all, because they pointed to something true. He and Dyson went on to explain to Jack that Christianity was a "true myth," containing the elements Jack loved in the pagan myths "but with this tremendous difference that it *really happened*: and one must be content to accept it in the same way, remembering that it is God's myth where the others are men's myths."[9] Their perspective and their words changed something fundamental for Jack. He did not convert on the spot, but nine days later he suddenly realized that he had come to believe not just in God but in Christ.

Jack may have been, as he later wrote, "the most dejected and reluctant convert in all England."[10] But after his conversion, he quickly and fully came to embrace the Christian faith. To compare Jack's writings, both public and private, before and after his conversion is to witness the incredible transforming power of Christ; hardly a corner of his mind or spirit remained untouched by the change. The once-pessimistic young poet can hardly be recognized in the cheerful, kindly figure that emerged. Though Jack, as his closest friends have reported, could still be (and very often was) fiercely combative in an intellectual debate or even a social situation, there was at the same time a new gentleness, patience, and generosity about him.

But as mentioned before, one of the biggest things that changed was the subject matter of much of his writing. *The Pilgrim's Regress*, published in 1933, was a book that, through allegory, traced the story of his return to the faith of his childhood. Though it did not sell well, future popular-level works on faith, beginning with *The Problem of Pain* (1940), would sell very well indeed. As it turned out, the belief that Jack had fought so long and hard against would not only transform his mind and soul but also bring him undreamed-of renown as a writer. (In another sign of just how sincerely he had come to believe, he gave away all the money he earned for his religious writings to charity.)

A Fan Letter and a Request

So Dorothy L. Sayers and C. S. Lewis were now frequently writing on similar subjects. But we can't point to a precise moment when Dorothy first became aware of Jack's work, or he of hers. All we know for sure is that their names started showing up in each other's writings in 1941. In letters to various correspondents, Dorothy recommends *The Problem of Pain* and occasionally also *The Allegory of Love*.[11] More than that, she quotes from both of these books in her own *The Mind of the Maker*.

In turn, we learn from one of Jack's letters to his old friend Arthur Greeves that he had read *The Mind of the Maker*—whether because he was quoted in it or because he was simply interested in the subject, Jack doesn't specify. He liked it so much that it led him to try *Gaudy Night*—but that one was too much for him. He was not a fan of detective stories, as he admitted to Greeves, and it left him cold.[12]

Gaudy Night, a novel that combines mystery, romance, and a love letter to Oxford, is a book so deeply beloved by its multitudes of fans that it's almost impossible for us to conceive of anyone not liking it, particularly when that person generally has excellent literary taste. (Incidentally, both Jack's brother and Jack's future wife would become great fans of Dorothy's mysteries!) We can at least give Jack credit for acknowledging that the problem was simply his dislike of the genre—though that's hard for some of us to understand as well!—and for not letting distaste for the book lead to a feeling of revulsion against its author.

By contrast, his friend Tolkien, who had enjoyed the earlier Peter Wimsey novels, wrote that when reading *Gaudy Night*, "I conceived a loathing for [Peter] (and his creatrix) not surpassed by any other character in literature known to me, unless by his Harriet."[13] Apparently Tolkien took literature very personally. But it should be noted that this particular novel was something of a departure from the previous books in the series. It was, more than any other, the novel in which Dorothy fully fleshed out her detective hero and her other characters—a little disconcerting for some of the fans who had most enjoyed Peter in his early, more Bertie Wooster–like phase. It was the novel in which she brought Harriet Vane, a character originally introduced as Peter's love interest, center stage, making her the focus of the action and the character whose inner life is most deeply explored. And it was, most of all, the novel in which Dorothy most fully expressed her ideas about the value and importance of women being able to pursue their intellectual interests and generally do the work they felt called to do. These were not themes that were likely to gain an enthusiastic hearing from academic gentlemen in the 1930s (especially since Dorothy took the opportunity to poke a little gentle fun at some of the hidebound types who were still upset by the presence of women in universities!).

At any rate, Dorothy, for her part, appears to have liked everything of Jack Lewis's that she was reading—so much so that sometime in early 1942, as we have seen, she wrote him a letter. Unfortunately, the letter has been lost, so we don't know exactly what she said to him, or how she said it, at this first epistolary encounter. We don't even know which work (or works) of his she was praising.

We do know, though, that she had him in mind to write for Bridgeheads, a series of books by Christian writers she was helping to plan and edit. It's not definite whether she asked him to do this in the original fan letter or in another letter after that.

Sayers's biographer Catherine Kenney explains that the Bridgeheads series "was dedicated to exploring the predicament in which England found itself in the early 1940s and to considering ways to restoring it after the war." She quotes Dorothy's "statement of aims" for the series as follows: "Our aim is to give the people of this country a constructive purpose worth living for and worth dying for."[14] It was a statement that managed to be simultaneously grand and practical, but then Dorothy L. Sayers had never lost her taste for either grandeur or practicality.

The Mind of the Maker was the first book in the Bridgeheads series. It's significant that it took a global crisis for Dorothy to write it and to encourage other writers to produce books like it. Christian though she was, she did not really consider herself an apologist at this time—and, as we'll see, it would never be a role she took to with great eagerness. It's very likely she didn't even consider this book a work of straight apologetics, with its application of the truths of Christianity to art and creativity. Not all the writers asked to write for the Bridgeheads series were Christians, so it may not even have occurred to her to look at her own project through that lens.

But as both a Christian and a British citizen during wartime, Dorothy took her duty to God and country seriously. (In fact, she and two of her closest friends, Helen Simpson and Muriel St. Clare Byrne—the latter of whom coedited the Bridgeheads series with Sayers—served on the Ministry of Information's Authors' Planning Committee.[15])

Beyond that, she could see all too clearly how her fellow Christians as well as her fellow British citizens had fallen short in the years leading up to World War II and how they had unwittingly contributed to the terrible state in which the world now found itself. Spiritually, economically, and in every other way, they had failed. She hoped to make an effort that would not only help sustain the country through the war but help society rebuild itself on a firmer basis afterward. This was her "war work," as the broadcast talks and speeches to the troops were Jack Lewis's.

It was a noble goal, but the project didn't quite come off. Only half of the six authors picked for the project were able to follow through on their commitment—and of the Bridgeheads books, only *The Mind of the Maker* is still widely remembered today. As for the book that Dorothy had in mind for Jack to write, that never even got off the ground. But that she wanted him to write it shows her high opinion of his theological understanding and writing ability—a great compliment, coming from a more established and famous writer, not to mention from someone who had been a Christian for much longer than Jack had.

Though we don't have the letter with her request, his answer shows that she had asked him to write on the subject of love and marriage. Walter Hooper states that Dorothy got the idea from Letter 18 in *The Screwtape Letters*, which deals with that subject, and which she thought contained (in Hooper's words) "much good sense."[16]

Letter 18 doesn't go into great depth on the topic; it simply makes the point that commitment in marriage must be based on something deeper than emotion. The response that Jack sent to Dorothy's letter throws some light on precisely which aspect of the subject she had asked him to write about. It begins:

> *Dear Miss Sayers—*
>
> *But why not write the book yourself? Either a novel, in which the familiar contrast of love-and-marriage versus career is replaced by the new (or so old as to be called new) contrast of love-and-misery versus happiness and marriage without "Love". Or a treatise. . . . I hope you'll do the novel. It wd. soften the blow. Because the job is difficult. One will be accused (and in a sense not untruly) of defending simple appetite against grand passion.*[17]

Difficult though the job may have been, the idea Jack was expressing here was one that Dorothy could fully endorse; her own tumultuous love life had taught her both the difficulty and the importance of managing romantic emotions and their need to be supported by something deeper. Both Jack and Dorothy, in fact, had good reason to understand the problems with unregulated feelings, and it's worth taking a moment to explore why.

Entanglements

Lewis's turn to faith marked a great change in his sexual values as in most of his other values; in the years before that, some of the tastes he expressed had been, to say the least, unorthodox. In the years before his conversion, he confided to Arthur Greeves more than once that he had sadomasochistic fantasies, even signing some of his letters "Philomastix," Greek for "fond of the whip."[18]

Another part of Lewis's life that's more widely known—but more mysterious—is his relationship with Janie King Moore, the mother of Paddy Moore, a good friend of Jack's who had died in World War I. Jack and Paddy had promised each other that, if either of them should die in the war, the other would care for his bereft parent. Jack, who had already come to know and like Mrs. Moore during her son's lifetime, would fulfill his promise to the extent of moving in with Mrs. Moore and her daughter, Maureen (along with his brother, Warren). The arrangement lasted until age and illness forced Mrs. Moore to go to a nursing home in 1950.

Biographers and scholars have long argued, and probably will argue until the end of time, over whether Jack and Mrs. Moore were actually lovers or only lived as mother and son. Plenty of solid arguments on both sides have been made. But given that he often referred to her as his mother, if there *was* a sexual relationship, the situation was almost too Freudian even for Freud.* Whatever the nature of their relationship, the consensus is that it was strongly influenced by their respective losses: Jack's loss of his mother and Mrs. Moore's loss of her son. Each found something in the other that provided some healing for old wounds and fulfillment of deep emotional needs, at least for a time.

In any event, after he converted to Christianity, Jack made it clear that he now fully endorsed and abided by the church's teachings on sexuality. Until he married, much later in life, he would practice celibacy. He would also continue to live with and take care of Mrs. Moore, however, even as she grew more difficult and demanding over the years. When she had to go to the nursing home late in life, he visited her daily. He always credited her with teaching him to be generous. But after her death in 1951, he confessed in a letter to one of his correspondents, Mary Van Deusen, that his life to that point had been full of "senseless wranglings, lyings, backbitings, follies, and *scares*. I never went home without a feeling of terror as to what appalling situation might have developed in my absence."[19] The recollections of Jack's brother, Warren, and of several others who knew Mrs. Moore corroborate this picture of her.

As for Dorothy, though she had never left her faith behind as Jack had, she had nonetheless given in to sexual temptation. She hadn't meant to at first; in fact, during an intense romance with Russian novelist John Cournos in her late twenties, she had stayed determinedly chaste, though

*In fact, Freud himself questions Lewis about the nature of the relationship in the 2009 play *Freud's Last Session* by Mark St. Germain, which presents a fictional meeting between Lewis and the pioneering psychologist. When he does, Lewis—just as he did in life—refuses to address the matter.

she had hinted to him that she might give in to his efforts at persuasion if only he would agree to marry her and have children with her. This he utterly refused to do, claiming that he did not believe in marriage. She in turn was repulsed by his arguments in favor of birth control, insisting that, for her, to love a man meant wanting to have his children. At last there was a bitter breakup.

On the rebound, Dorothy threw herself into a relationship with a man who could not possibly have been more different from the highbrow and arrogant Cournos: an unemployed car salesman named Bill White, with a wife from whom he was estranged.[20] This time Dorothy did give in to persuasion—and became pregnant. (Even though now she was using birth control after all!)

To the understandably confused Cournos—who by now had married someone else—Dorothy wrote, "Both of us did what we swore we'd never do, you see."[21] In a later letter, she reiterated her point of view. "The one thing worse than bearing the child of a man you hate would be being condemned to be childless by the man you loved."[22]

It was, perhaps, an unusual principle for a twentieth-century woman who in many ways was a woman of her time. But Dorothy had quite a few unusual principles—things she considered a matter of integrity while the rest of her world wasn't quite in step with her and couldn't figure out her stubbornness on the matter. In this case, perhaps wanting to explain or justify herself further, she would give her fictional heroine, Harriet Vane, similarly unusual and unfashionable principles about marriage. (Harriet agrees to live with a man who, like Cournos, says he doesn't believe in marriage; when he does propose to her, she rejects him, feeling that he had tricked her just to see if her "devotion was abject enough." "I didn't like having matrimony offered as a bad-conduct prize," Harriet explains to the detective-hero Lord Peter Wimsey, who signals his worthiness of her by being one of the few people who truly understands what she's getting at.[23])

Dorothy's way of handling the pregnancy was equally unusual: she kept her child a lifelong secret from most people she knew, including her parents. At the age of thirty, she was hardly a wayward teenager terrified of her family, but still, "it's not the kind of ill-doing that Mother has any sympathy for," she told her cousin Ivy Shrimpton.[24] She knew her parents, sympathetic and supportive as they had always been, nonetheless would be disappointed in her, and she wanted to protect them, and probably also herself, from that disappointment. Dorothy gave birth to her son, John Anthony, in a private maternity home in January 1924, and when he was just a few weeks old, he went to live with Ivy and her mother, Dorothy's Aunt Amy, who fostered children for a living.*

In terms of her spiritual life, perhaps the pregnancy was the best thing that could have happened to Dorothy at this point. It brought her up short, ended the affair with White, who left for good not long after the baby's birth, and forced her to be honest with herself and with God about the nature of her actions.

Barbara Reynolds, in her biography, offers a helpful way of looking at Dorothy's Christian faith in relation to this situation.

---

*As Barbara Reynolds explains, "Such arrangements had been regularised by the Act of 1908, which protected infants maintained for pay by foster parents. Aunt Amy and Ivy were no baby-farmers. Their little charges thrived and were well taught" (*Dorothy L. Sayers: Her Life and Soul*, 123).

She was an Anglo-Catholic* and . . . it was her practice to go to confession. . . . Whenever it was that she entered into a state of repentance, her recourse then was to make confession and seek absolution. When she did so, the burden of guilt was lifted. . . . What remained for her was a burden of responsibility. In practical terms, this meant supporting and educating John Anthony and providing him, as best she could, with maternal love and concern for his welfare.[25]

This passage indicates another reason that she lived apart from her son, besides the desire to keep him a secret: she had to provide for him financially, and she had little faith in her own ability to work and raise a child at the same time, especially in a period where her situation was relatively rare and would be looked down upon. In addition to writing novels, she was working full-time at an advertising agency. "Didn't even have to chuck my job!" she wrote triumphantly to Cournos about her success in hiding her pregnancy—also signifying just why it might be so necessary for a single working woman to do such a thing in 1920s England.[26]

Dorothy kept up a lively correspondence with Ivy over John Anthony's well-being, and went to see him when she could, but during her lifetime she posed as someone who had simply taken an interest in a child her cousin was fostering and was contributing to his welfare. (When he was ten years old, the boy would be told that "Cousin Dorothy" had officially adopted him, though he continued to live with Ivy.)

A couple of years after her son's birth, in 1926, Dorothy met and married journalist and World War I veteran Oswald Atherton "Mac" Fleming, a divorced man twelve years her

*See footnote on p. 41 about the usage of the term *catholic* here.

senior. Though she wasn't madly in love with Mac, Dorothy welcomed the stability that he at first brought to her life and enjoyed him as a sexual partner. (But not wanting any more children, she again used birth control. As sometimes happens after one has worn oneself out defending a principle, the principle suddenly collapsed. Or maybe it didn't; maybe her husband simply was not a man she longed to have children with.) Mac even offered to adopt her son, though ultimately he did not follow through. He did, however, allow John Anthony to use his own last name of Fleming.

The marriage, as mentioned earlier, would grow more and more difficult as Mac's war-related physical and mental illnesses grew worse, somewhat mirroring what Jack was going through with Mrs. Moore. (Mac's first marriage had dissolved in large part because "his personality had changed, as though he had been damaged psychologically by the war," and he had "cut himself off from his wife and family."[27]) But Dorothy, like Jack, stayed loyal to the commitment she had made. She was a faithful wife to Mac, though they often quarreled bitterly, and took care of him until his death in 1950.

First Meeting

In her 1926 novel *Clouds of Witness,* one of Dorothy's recurring characters, the wise lawyer Sir Impey Biggs, quips, "Time and trouble will tame an advanced young woman, but an advanced old woman is uncontrollable by any earthly force."[28] By the time she wrote those words, trouble had tamed Dorothy Sayers—at least, as much as she was capable of being tamed. As they began their correspondence in 1942, both she and Jack brought to the subject of sexuality a clear understanding of and commitment to the teachings of the church, backed up by experiences and memories that had taught them something about the great value of those teachings.

Yet Jack never did write the Bridgeheads book Dorothy wanted him to write. Part of the reason for this was that the enthusiasm she expressed in her letter convinced him that she should be the one to write it instead! Clearly he was not yet aware of just how easily and how often Dorothy L. Sayers could get enthusiastic. He insisted—to the point that it started to become almost comic—that she sounded like she was "straining at the leash" to write the book herself.[29] But he did ask her to come to Oxford and have lunch with him in early June to talk about the project.

So it appears likely that Dorothy L. Sayers and C. S. Lewis finally met in person on either June 2 or 3 of 1942 (the dates that he suggested to her in his invitation). Though we don't have her response to his letter, since Dorothy was so eager to talk more with Jack about the project, it's probable that their first meeting did take place then. Unfortunately, since neither participant seems to have left any record of this meeting, we don't know for certain that it took place, or, if it did, how it went! But in any event, this period began a shift from a casual and admiring acquaintance to a genuine friendship.

The letters that follow are, at first, somewhat sporadic. The first of these that we have is from October 1942, from Jack to Dorothy (though it makes clear that he is answering an earlier letter from her, which has apparently been lost). But their correspondence already has taken on the tone of letters between friends, full of jokes, recommendations, opinions, and dialogues on subjects ranging from Virgil to Milton to Shakespeare to T. S. Eliot.

That last figure was one whom Jack never quite warmed up to as a poet (even though he eventually would come to like him as a person), and he was not shy about saying so. "Oh Eliot! How can a man who is neither a knave nor a fool write so like both?" Jack laments in that October letter (apropos of what, we don't know). "Well, he can't complain that I haven't done my best to put him right—hardly ever write a book without showing him one of his errors. And still he doesn't mend. I call it ungrateful."[30]

Characteristically, in this letter Jack combines passionate opinions on literature with a light, even playful tone. It appears that he had recognized in Dorothy someone with whom he could banter about favorite subjects, as he loved to do with his own circle of friends. This is not to say that he and Dorothy had instantly become fast friends; their friendship was still in its very early stages. But it signifies that, even at this early stage, they were comfortable and at ease with each other.

The Sluckdrib Letter

We know that Dorothy kept up her end of the correspondence over the next year, from reading Jack's responses to what she wrote, but the first letter that we actually have from her to him is dated May 13, 1943. This letter shares the simultaneous gravity and playfulness of his letters to her. It is, in fact, her own version of a Screwtape letter, purportedly penned by a demon called Sluckdrib, who was Sayers's own "Personal Attendant."

A number of writers have tried their hand at imitating *The Screwtape Letters* in format, viewpoint, and tone in the decades since the book was published. In this author's opinion, no others have come close to Dorothy L. Sayers's version, for a few reasons. One is Dorothy's sheer literary brilliance. She may have been best known as a writer of detective stories—and detective stories that were underappreciated by Jack, at that!—but she wrote them uncommonly well, with a depth of characterization and a skill in descriptive writing and mood setting (especially in her later novels) that were rare even among the best writers of the Golden Age of detective fiction. And in her essays, plays, and nonfiction books like *The Mind of the Maker*, her considerable intellectual and literary gifts were fully on display. As scholar Christine A. Colón notes, in examining the high level of skill and artistry that Sayers brought to even her "middlebrow" work, "The lessons she had learned as she worked to perfect the craft of the detective novel would continue to serve her well as she transitioned into other genres."[31] Small wonder, then, that she could succeed so well at imitating the work of another brilliant writer.

The second reason Dorothy's pastiche succeeds is that—unlike many that came after it—she took Jack's format and style wholly seriously and submitted herself to their requirements, rather than attempting to bend his creation to suit her own style and purposes, as too many other would-be imitators have done. And the third reason is that—again, unlike so many others who have tried it—Dorothy is not adapting this style just to mock the foibles of her age; she is chiefly using it to mock her own foibles. Her "demon" refers to Dorothy as a "fifth-rate soul . . . thoroughly worm-eaten and shaky," and gleefully reels off a whole list of faults and bad habits brought on by the writing of *The Man Born to*

Be King, from "intellectual and spiritual pride" to "neglect of domestic affairs."[32] Her frank humility was a quality that Jack took particular notice of, and would continue to notice in the ensuing years.

The situation Dorothy describes in the Sluckdrib letter is her own correspondence with an atheist named L. T. Duff. (This is the same correspondence mentioned in the introduction to this book. At the end of this letter, Dorothy drops the Sluckdrib persona and writes the portion of the letter we saw there, about how she didn't like souls.) In the letter, her personal tempter rejoices that the correspondence is bringing out the worst in Dorothy. "I saw to it," Sluckdrib boasts, "that her motive was mere pride and self-sufficiency, not in the least contaminated by 'love' for the Atheist or interest in 'saving' his moth-eaten soul."[33]

Yet in another part of the letter, the tempter laments that, despite all this, the correspondence seems to be having what she considers an alarming effect on both the atheist *and* Dorothy: "What is so sinister is his growing good-will (which is beginning to affect my patient). . . . He does not see the despicable meanness of her motives, which is enough to make a cat sick."[34]

Like Jack's earlier letters to her, Dorothy's letter to him both captures much of her own personality and points to issues and ideas that would be important in their forthcoming correspondence: integrity, artistry, evangelism, and the way in which these various qualities and callings might end up interfering with each other. Despite their different temperaments, priorities, and ideas about how to handle these matters, they both had strong and lively intellects, a love and understanding of literature, and faith in God—at a time and place when the first two did not always go hand in hand with the third. Both of them, in addition, had a gift for friendship, a genuine appreciation of its importance, and a genius for finding people with whom they could wholeheartedly share it.

Through these commonalities they were beginning to build a connection that would prove vital to them both. But as so often happens in the course of friendship, once they had discovered their similarities, they would next have to reckon with some of their differences.

Three

"Hey! Whoa!"

A Conflict

Although Jack and Dorothy had hit it off so well, their letters to each other over the next three years or so appear to have been relatively infrequent. I use the word *appear* because, given Lewis's habit of throwing letters away, it's difficult to know for sure how many there were. That he eventually did start keeping Dorothy's letters is another indication of how highly he regarded her abilities as a letter writer, as well as the steady growth of their friendship. As Marjorie Lamp Mead, associate director of the Marion E. Wade Center, points out, "Lewis did not keep letters . . . but hers [to him] exist."[1] But at this early stage, with their relationship still mainly on a professional footing, it's not surprising (though unfortunate for us) that they wrote each other few letters and that Jack may not have kept all that Dorothy did send.

This early correspondence consisted in large part of sending each other copies of their work, and the resulting praise and critiques. He delighted in her essay "The Other Six Deadly Sins" (in which she was rather biting on the subject of the church acting as if there were only one deadly sin, the sin of lust),[2] and he told her that he had "shed real tears (hot ones)" while reading the printed version of *The Man Born to Be King* she had sent him.[3] He would read it many more times in the years to come, eventually making the rereading a regular Lenten practice. For her part, she wrote to him that she thought *That Hideous Strength* was "tremendously full of good things." Although she confessed that Ransom, its hero, had begun to irritate her "since he took to being golden-haired and interesting on a sofa like the Heir of Redclyffe," she was full of praise for numerous other characters and scenes.[4]

On the rare occasions when one disliked one of the other's works—as he did with her play *The Zeal of Thy House* and she did with much of *Mere Christianity*—they said little or nothing to each other about it, sharing their opinions only with other friends.[5] But as long as there was something to praise as well as to criticize, they would freely offer both praise and criticism to each other.

Essays Presented to Charles Williams

In 1945 an opportunity arose for Jack and Dorothy to work together for the first time—an opportunity arising out of a sad occasion for both of them. Their mutual friend Charles Williams died suddenly and unexpectedly on May 15 of that year.

Though not an academic—he worked for the Oxford University Press—Williams was a gifted and esoteric writer of poetry and supernatural thrillers who had been invited to join the Inklings when his company moved from London to

Oxford for the duration of World War II. His work and his friendship had been an enormous influence on Jack Lewis— just how enormous is suggested by the fact that, even before his death, Jack had already been planning to compile, edit, and publish a volume of essays by various writers in Williams's honor, in anticipation of his being sent back to London by his company after the war. (Tolkien was helping with the project; he considered Williams a friend, although he was not nearly as big a fan of Williams's work as Jack was.)

Williams's influence on Dorothy L. Sayers had been, if possible, even greater than his influence on Lewis. They had first met after Williams sent an admiring letter about Dorothy's novel *The Nine Tailors* (1934) to her publisher, and her publisher forwarded the letter on to Dorothy. It was Williams who inspired Dorothy to read Dante Alighieri, the poet who was to become the driving force of her work. Williams had also helped her get the commission to write *The Zeal of Thy House*, her first Canterbury play.

As she embarked on her own translation of Dante's *Divine Comedy*, Dorothy considered Williams her mentor and guide, seizing eagerly on his insights about the poet's beliefs, techniques, and style. She tentatively (as tentatively as she could do anything) sent him her translation of the first five cantos, and it was his praise and encouragement that stimulated her to keep going with it. When she began to talk with E. V. Rieu, editor of the Penguin Classics series, about publishing the translation, she extracted a promise from Williams to write some sort of preface or introduction for it. She was, of course, shocked and devastated to hear of his death.

When Jack wrote to offer Dorothy the chance to contribute to the volume of essays to be dedicated to Williams—now a memorial volume, with the proceeds earmarked for Williams's widow—she grasped at the opportunity to write an essay arising out of her extensive correspondence with Williams on Dante, something that Williams himself had strongly urged her to do sometime. Though she sent the piece with multiple apologies for its length, Jack liked it, on the whole (though he privately confided to fellow Inkling Owen Barfield that it was "perhaps a trifle vulgar in places").[6] He was happy to include it in the book, which was ultimately titled *Essays Presented to Charles Williams*.

Incidentally, a few years after publication, a copy of the book made its way to Joy Davidman—the New York writer who would one day play such a crucial role in Jack's life—who liked Jack's and Dorothy's essays the best of all of those included, and recorded that the latter "sent me tearing off to read Dante"—exactly the kind of response Dorothy would have hoped for![7]

This collaboration helped to get Jack's and Dorothy's correspondence going more routinely—and incidentally, it also offered Jack a better look at the "zesty" side of Dorothy's personality. A misunderstanding with Oxford University Press, the prospective publisher of the book, led Jack to tell Dorothy, mistakenly, that the head of the company had asked that the writers pay for the publishing costs of the volume.

At the suggestion of such an unorthodox and unprofessional arrangement, Dorothy exploded. "Good God Almighty! And Charles served that firm faithfully for nearly all his life! . . . Does that comic little man expect ME to pay for the privilege of being published by him? *Pay*? PAY?—Or, if it comes to that, YOU? Most publishers," she added, with entire truth, "would be pretty glad to have our names on their lists at any price."[8]

Dorothy wasn't just throwing a tantrum or trying to pull rank as a celebrity. Lack of professionalism and disrespect for authors had always infuriated her. At one point during the writing of *The Man Born to Be King*, she had literally torn up her contract with the BBC when an assistant director had tried to assert a right to edit her plays before production, rather than waiting for the rehearsal period to make suggestions as was customary with dramatic productions. Needless to say, Dorothy won that battle.

But as it turned out, no such drastic actions were needed this time. Jack had already written to OUP—in a considerably milder tone—to protest. He was soon able to forward Dorothy their response, which cleared up the misunderstanding and assured them that the publishers would bear the expense of publication, accompanied by a note of his own, which read in part: "Best quality Sackcloth & Ashes in sealed packets delivered in plain vans at moderate charges."[9]

Dorothy's repentance for her rage was, in its way, as emphatic as the rage itself had been. She wrote back to Jack:

> *My menu tonight shall be:*
>
> *HUMBLE PIE*
> *IPISSIMA VERBA**
> *with sharp sauce*
> *FRUITS*
> *meet for Repentance*
>
> *I take it all back, including "comic little man."*[10]

*A Latin term meaning "the very words," suggesting that Dorothy was eating her words.

But even if their collaboration on the Williams project hadn't occurred, it was probably inevitable that Dorothy and Jack would eventually begin seeking each other out for help and advice. The popularity of their spiritual writings had left both of them similarly situated: they were now considered go-to consultants on religious topics by publishers, the media, and the general public. Neither felt quite prepared for the role, and each may have felt a little isolated in it. As mentioned earlier, Jack's work in apologetics had won him few fans at Oxford, and though he had the friendship and loyalty of the Inklings, none of them were engaged in quite the same kind of work and thus could not fully understand what it was like. The same was true of most of Dorothy's friends.

But both felt compelled to try to do what they could—although their reactions to being asked, and their thoughts on what the scope of their role should be, often differed widely. It was small wonder that they started to turn to each other more and more to discuss the unique challenges of that role, even though their differences would sometimes lead to clashes.

"The Artistic Conscience"

Despite the reluctance often revealed in her letters, Dorothy was conscientiously filling the part she saw for herself as an advocate for the role of Christian faith and principles in rebuilding the postwar society—to an extent that had, unbeknownst to her, been rather too much for Charles Williams. According to his biographer Grevel Lindop, Williams "grumbled about being press-ganged into 'Dorothy Sayers's committees for explaining or defending or promulgating or elucidating or doing something or other to the Faith.'"[11]

Yet for all that, Dorothy was determined, in modern parlance, to stay in her lane, addressing only those matters she felt well qualified and inclined to address. It was a matter of integrity for her, one that went far beyond mere likes and tastes. She had a positive horror of bad work done in a good cause, believing fervently that it did no good and much harm. And she was convinced that any kind of creative work undertaken solely for the purpose of edification could not help but turn bad. (It's regrettable that we can't hear her opinions on, say, the state of modern Christian filmmaking.)

She felt that Jack, by contrast, was a little too prone to step outside his area of expertise, albeit usually out of a sincere conviction that someone of the Christian persuasion had to say *something* about whatever was being discussed. Even when he was reluctant to speak up on an issue, he could often be persuaded if enough pressure was applied. Dorothy strenuously resisted whenever she thought he was attempting to persuade her to do the same thing—and it wasn't long before she demonstrated just how strenuous she could be. While Jack had, if anything, encouraged her fit of temper over the Williams project ("That's the spirit!"[12]), at least until he discovered his mistake in the matter, he was about to find out what it was like to have the full force of the gale turned upon him.

This conversation is worth exploring in detail, even aside from what it reveals about their personalities and relationships.[13] It throws light on what for many Christians is a perennial problem: the role of art and creativity in our lives and how it relates to faith. Specifically, should artists create art to communicate a message—such as the gospel message—or should they create art simply because they were called to create art and let it speak for itself? It was a question Dorothy L. Sayers had thought through carefully. Her ideas on artistic integrity had been expressed throughout her work, from *Gaudy Night* to *The Zeal of Thy House* to *The Mind of the Maker*. It was, in short, a matter she felt quite passionate about.

In July 1946, Jack Lewis wrote to tell her that he was planning to write something for a book series meant as "a sort of library of Christian knowledge for young people," and to ask if she would be willing to do so as well. "Don't blast me," he ended the letter, somewhat prophetically. "Good books *have* sometimes been begotten by letters like this!"[14]

Dorothy did not blast him—yet. She did turn him down, explaining that (in Reynolds's paraphrase) "her conscience prevented her from writing for the purpose of edifying readers."[15] Jack made an attempt at talking her around with a mixture of understanding and judiciously applied flattery.

I also am haunted at times by the feeling that I oughtn't to be doing this kind of thing. But as the voice, when interrogated, can never give a good reason, I doubt if it comes from above. . . . I wish I knew what place artistic consciences will hold a moment after death. It might be—and then it might be exactly the reverse. You write such excellent letters that if I were a bad man, I should lure you into an epistolary controversy and you wd. find you had written a book for us without knowing it: I shd. simply publish the letters.[16]

Dorothy was not having it. To do the kind of thing he was asking, she insisted, was to tell a lie, and "in the end the lie rots inwards and corrupts the art itself." She continued, paraphrasing T. S. Eliot, "You must not do even the right deed for the wrong reason."[17]

> You must not accept money, you must not accept applause, you must not accept a "following," you must not accept even the assurance that you are doing good as an excuse for writing anything but the thing you want to say. . . . You must not tell people what they want to hear, or even what they need to hear, unless it is the thing you passionately want to tell them.[18]

She went so far as to assert that "an awful judgment" awaited those who practiced such dishonesty in their art.

> The false thing *may*—I only say *may*—assist a few souls here and now, but God knows how many it may help to damn at another time. Take shoddy, weak, sentimental religious art: there are pious souls who get comfort out of bad stained glass and sloppy hymns and music (though they might well have got better nourishment out of honest stuff). But thousands of others have spewed at the sight and sound of it, and said "If Christianity fosters that kind of thing it must have a lie in its soul." No, you can't divide the conscience into "artistic" and the other sort. It's all one; and you can't serve God with lies: whether the lie is in the intention or in the workmanship is no odds—it will eat its way right through in the end.[19]

It was an issue that Jack had wrestled with himself, and Dorothy picked up on that. The regard she had for him, despite the difference of opinion, shows in the way she softened her tone a little at the end of the letter, something she would not have done for everyone. She urged him to take a break from his apologetic work if he was feeling at all doubtful about it or drained by it, trusting that such a break would refresh and restore his appetite for the work. Then she finished her letter:

> *If I have been impertinent, please forgive me. You didn't scold me as vigorously as I expected, and I just wondered. Yours tentatively (how do you like that?),*
>
> Dorothy L. Sayers[20]

Jack thanked her for the "intensely interesting letter," but still was not quite convinced.

> Of course one mustn't do *dishonest* work. But you seem to take as the criterion of honest work the sensible *desire* to write, the "itch." That seems to me precious like making "being in love" the only reason for going on with a marriage.[21]

Perhaps he had made this comparison because writing something on that very subject of love and marriage had been her first request to him. It may be that he thought that mentioning a topic on which he knew they had some common ground—and moreover, obliquely reminding her that she had done her own share of asking him to write this or that—would calm things down.

If so, he could not have been more wrong. In response to his one-paragraph letter came a flurry of exasperated pages. Jack had unwittingly touched a nerve, and now he was in for it.

In this letter, Dorothy dove deep into what she saw as the difference between proclaiming the truth that God had given her to proclaim and trying to write something to order based solely on "spiritual experience," which she thought he was trying to encourage her to do. All such experiences, she declared, were "a closed book" to her and always had been.

"That is why," she wrote, "I am obliged to resent and resist this religious racket which is continually forcing me into false situations—urging me to write on subjects which I cannot honestly handle, or distorting what I do say in a manner which makes me appear to lay claim to more 'faith' and 'spirituality' than I have." She chastised Jack for calling her convictions on the matter nothing but an "itch." And she went on to make a point that is still startlingly fresh; though she could not have foreseen the relentless celebrity machine of modern evangelical culture, it seems she had experienced a taste of it already.

It does seem to me that all you religious people [an interesting formulation, given that she and Jack both professed Christianity] *trust* God so little. You can't wait to see what He wants to do with a soul or a talent. You must drag the eggs out of the goose before the shell's on, or dig up the plant to teach it to grow. No sooner does some poor mutt announce, "I've found a bit of truth", than you're all round like daughters of the horse-leech:* "Go on, hand it out! Exploit the vein! It's your *duty* to go on talking!" By the bones of Balaam's ass, it is no such thing. When the time comes

*A reference to Proverbs 30:15, "The leech has two daughters—Give and Give!" (NKJV).

to speak, we shall speak, since that is what we are made for. In the meantime it's no good beating us or shouting at us till we can't hear what communication is trying to come over.[22]

"Hey! Whoa!" Jack protested.[23] A veteran of many a fiery intellectual and spiritual debate, he knew when he was beaten, but he made one last valiant attempt at defending the purity of his motives and actions. He assured Dorothy that he hadn't meant to urge her to do anything she didn't want to do, and that he didn't actually disagree with her—only that, as he had said before, he tended to doubt his own wisdom on the subject.

"I apologise for having got so hot," Dorothy replied.

In fact, in your prophetic moments, you are with me—that is, if the corrupt artist in *The Great Divorce* is in Hell *because* he is a corrupt artist. He has turned from serving the work and making the work serve him, and no longer paints because he is summoned to express and communicate, but for some other reason. And I don't think it matters very much what, or how specious, the other reason is. . . . The only rule I can find is to write what you feel impelled to write, and let God do what He likes with the stuff.[24]

There (after a few more paragraphs in a similar vein) the matter rested. The two of them were still working on the Williams project at this point, and the work went on as before, though Jack could not resist the opportunity to tease Dorothy a bit in a later letter, after she had apparently asked him to stand up for her with the printers: "The idea of *my* being stern with printers on your behalf is at once comic and alarming, seeing as how everyone knows that butter won't melt in my mouth and you inspire a wholesome terror, I'm told, in all publishers, printers, producers, journalists, etc."[25]

It isn't clear whether Dorothy's outburst really cleared up any and all doubts that Jack felt on the role of edification in art, or the duty of the Christian artist. However, some of his later writings do reflect more confidence in his point of view on these matters. Take, for instance, the essay "On Three Ways of Writing for Children," written after he had become a successful children's author with *The Lion, the Witch and the Wardrobe*. In this essay, he rejected the idea that a good children's story could begin with an author asking the question, What do modern children need? "If we ask that question," he wrote,

> we are assuming too superior an attitude. . . . But it is better not to ask the questions at all. Let the pictures [in your mind] tell you their own moral. For the moral inherent in them will rise from whatever spiritual roots you have succeeded in striking during the whole course of your life. But if they don't show you any moral, don't put one in. For the moral you put in is likely to be a platitude, or even a falsehood, skimmed from the surface of your consciousness. . . . The only moral that is of any value is that which arises inevitably from the whole cast of the author's mind.[26]

Jack Lewis had a wide variety of influences in his life, and so one cannot say with certainty that he originally got this idea from Dorothy L. Sayers. If her own perceptions are to be believed, he had more or less held to the idea all along.

But at the very least, she may have helped to clear away some of his doubts on the subject and to put his convictions into words. There is more than a faint echo here of her own words to him about writing what one has been given to say instead of asking what people needed to hear. What is certain is that, if she ever read what he wrote here, she would have appreciated and approved of it.

What is also certain is that, far from damaging their friendship, this argument helped to solidify it. It signified to Dorothy that Jack was indeed a valuable friend, one to whom she could freely speak her mind without fear of reproach. Actually, it's worth asking if the dialogue can even be called an argument, despite Dorothy's vehemence. Jack had, in fact, done very little arguing—remarkably little for a man who was renowned among his colleagues, friends, and students for being able to turn even small talk into an argument. He had approached her diffidently, expressed his thoughts with only a mild persistence, and promptly backed down when he realized he was outgunned.

This may have been because, as he told her, he did not truly oppose her stance but merely felt uncomfortable fully adopting it. It's also possible that, since he was more used to arguing on intellectual topics with men than women, he may have felt a little unsure of how to handle himself, and consequently restrained himself more than usual. This is only speculation, as he did not actually express any such thoughts on the matter. But as much as he respected her and the other academic and professional women he knew, he did have some preconceptions about gender that might have hampered him from expressing himself with women the way he would have with his male friends. (His Oxford colleague and friend Kathleen

Lea claimed to know of at least one instance "when he could have wiped the floor with a young woman on a philosophical issue, and *did not*."[27]) Though he was not fully aware of it just yet, they were preconceptions that his friendship with Dorothy L. Sayers would do a great deal to alter.

Four

"A Complete Blank"

Of Men, Women, and Williams

Though Jack had what Dorothy considered the regrettable habit of weighing in on all sorts of topics, there were times when he recognized that she was better equipped to handle a task than he was. In July 1948, he wrote to let her know he was hearing rumors that the Anglican church was considering the ordination of women. He was against the idea, but thought that for him, a man, to publicly criticize it would be a mistake. He suggested that, if she too was against it, she should "write an article . . . and swear at me as much as you please while doing it."[1]

Dorothy sent back a letter that is still causing confusion to this day, even though she wrote as openly and straightforwardly as she usually did. As Kathryn Wehr observes in an article in VII: *Journal of the Marion E. Wade Center*, "Contemporary readers have sometimes sought implicit support for women priests in Sayers's opposition to the idea that only male priests could represent Christ."[2] And yet, if we look at the reference to the pro-ordination movement in the opening lines of Dorothy's letter—"Oh, lord! Look here, are you sure, of your own knowledge, that this precious 'movement' has any weight behind it?"[3]—she hardly seems to be aligning herself with it. Barbara Reynolds confirms in her biography, "I once asked her what she thought about this and she said in her opinion it was wisest to stick to traditional practice."[4]

Still, she was reluctant to write an article on the topic. She did say that she thought it would be a terrible idea "to erect a . . . barrier between us and the rest of Catholic Christendom" and to "break with Apostolic tradition," but she went on to say:

> I fear you would find me rather an uneasy ally. I can never find any logical or strictly theological reason against it. In so far as the Priest represents Christ, it is obviously more dramatically appropriate that a man should be, so to speak, cast for the part. But if I were cornered and asked point-blank whether Christ Himself is the representative of male humanity or all humanity, I should be obliged to answer "of all humanity"; and to cite the authority of St. Augustine for saying that woman also is made in the image of God.[5]

The best she could do, she concluded, was to keep silent on the subject.*

*After this discussion, Lewis would go ahead and write an essay on the subject himself, titled "Priestesses in the Church?" Interestingly, he included in it some of Sayers's points, warning that the ordination of women would "cut ourselves off from the Christian past and . . . widen the divisions between ourselves and other

Her choice of words in the passage above is significant. Her thoughts on the Christian doctrine of the *imago Dei*, or image of God, had a great bearing on her thoughts on gender. They led her in rather a different direction than either strictly traditionalist thinking or strictly feminist thinking would have taken her.

And her thoughts on gender, in turn, helped shape her relationships with and her very images of two of her closest male friends, Jack Lewis and Charles Williams. For this reason, it is worth taking a few moments at this point to explore what she (and Lewis) made of Williams—and what they missed about him.

A Guide and Mentor

Dorothy L. Sayers and Charles Williams became friends with each other several years before either became friends with Lewis, and it was this friendship, as we've seen, that led to one of the great passions of her life. Dorothy read Williams's book *The Figure of Beatrice*, which served as an introduction to Dante, in 1943. Her liking for that book motivated her, in August 1944, to grab her as-yet-unread copy of Dante's *Inferno* on her way to her backyard shelter during an air raid.

The experience of reading Dante electrified her like few other experiences in her life. "The plain fact is," she wrote later, "I bolted my meals, neglected my sleep, work and correspondence, drove my friends crazy, and paid only a distracted

Churches." Repr. http://www.episcopalnet.org/TRACTS/priestesses.html, accessed October 14, 2018.

attention to the doodle-bugs [German missiles] which happened to be infesting the neighborhood at the time," until she had finished reading the entire *Divine Comedy*.[6] She compared the experience to her first reading of *The Three Musketeers* at age thirteen, which had thoroughly captured her imagination and her affection. From her, there was no higher praise.

Almost the first thing she did after reading Dante's masterpiece was to write Charles Williams a lengthy and rapturous letter about it. It would be the first of many lengthy and rapturous letters about Dante that she would write, both to Williams and to others (including Jack Lewis). She considered Williams her mentor in all things related to Dante, to an extent that seems to have bemused him somewhat. After a visit from Sayers at the house where he was staying in Oxford, during which she kept him up and talking far into the night, Williams wrote to his wife, Florence "Michal" Williams, "I like the old dear, but she's rather heavy going."[7] ("Old dear" was an odd choice of expression, as Dorothy was seven years younger than he was.) The enthusiastic personality that for Jack Lewis was like "a high wind" seems to have bowled Williams over.

However, Williams had told Dorothy that her "naivety of approach" to Dante might be helpful to others who were interested in reading him but found themselves too intimidated to start. They would be able to relate to her experience and to the qualities she had discovered for herself in the great poet's work: chiefly, his ability to tell an exciting story.[8] Simply put, she would be able to help knock some of the rust off Dante for other prospective readers. When she wrote the essay for Williams's memorial volume, at Jack's request, she tried to do just that, and she would continue to use Williams's suggested approach to the subject in many future writings on Dante.

In a similar fashion, Jack found himself deeply influenced by Williams, to the point that many of his friends, including Dorothy, could trace Williams's ideas and imagery in Jack's work. For instance, the final scenes of *That Hideous Strength*, the third book of Jack's Space Trilogy, portray an eruption of the supernatural into the natural world very like the kind that Williams portrayed in his own novels. In a sense, Jack and Dorothy were once again sharing a guide, just as they had shared a guide in G. K. Chesterton all those years ago without knowing it. (Some have suggested that Elwin Ransom, the protagonist of the trilogy, who started out as a middle-aged philologist rather like Tolkien, actually evolves into a Williams-like figure by the third book, with an altered, more youthful appearance and a strange, entrancing power over people.[9] If so, it's odd that Dorothy—who, we'll recall, complained to Jack about the change in the character—didn't pick up on the resemblance.)

By all accounts, Williams was an exceptionally charismatic man with a strange ability to alter the atmosphere of a room just by walking into it, to make people feel better about themselves, and to make them admire him—sometimes almost to the point of literal worship. He had this powerful effect on numerous people besides Jack Lewis and Dorothy L. Sayers. But to account for the particular effect he had on Dorothy—who saw him in person less frequently than Jack and the other Inklings did—it helps to remember her particular context as a female writer and thinker in 1940s Britain.

Women and the *Imago Dei*

As a woman who had graduated from Oxford early in the twentieth century and had retained scholarly interests and ways of thinking—and furthermore, a woman who wrote for a living—Dorothy did not have a great deal of choice when it came to forming her friendships. She did have several close friends who were intellectual and creative women, some of whom, like Muriel St. Clare Byrne, she had known since college, and with whom she collaborated on various projects.[10] But at that time and in that place, in both her personal and professional lives, she needed male friends as well—both to network with and just to talk to about the things that interested her most.

In 1930, when Sayers helped form the prestigious Detection Club for mystery writers, the majority of the members were men (including G. K. Chesterton, the writer Dorothy had admired so much since adolescence). When planning the Bridgeheads series, she approached both male and female writers to be part of it. And to discuss Dante, she needed to talk to people, both men and women, who had studied Dante. "Unfortunately," she told Williams, "I have nobody to talk to here (my husband's comment would only be, 'What on earth do you want to read that stuff for?')."[11] She was positively desperate to share her enthrallment with someone who would understand.

There are many Christian leaders and thinkers, it's worth noting, who would point to Dorothy's words as a red flag. A married woman complaining to another man that her husband doesn't share her interests and forming a friendship with that other man based on shared intellectual pursuits—surely that's just asking for trouble.

Except it wasn't. When Dorothy wrote to Charles Williams and Jack Lewis and others that she was passionate about Dante and simply wanted to talk about him, she meant exactly what she said, no more and no less: she was passionate about Dante and simply wanted to talk about him. (Anyone familiar with her correspondence will bear witness to just *how* passionate she was. To read volumes 3 and 4 of Sayers's letters is to feel absolutely immersed in Dante.) Her marriage may have been less than satisfying, and she and Mac may have grown apart over the years—Barbara Reynolds recounts in her biography that back in 1933, Dorothy had considered a separation—but she was not looking for any new romantic interest.[12] She had made her commitment and, ultimately, she would follow through. If she could not share her excitement over Dante with her husband, she would seek outlets among her friends, that was all.*

Besides, it was what Dorothy referred to as "the passionate intellect" that was ultimately dominant in her life.[13] She had found that nothing else excited her quite like the life of the mind—and moreover, that any true passion must be influenced by, and regulated by, the head as well as the heart.

Back in 1935, she had put some of her thoughts and feelings on the subject into *Gaudy Night*. When Harriet Vane recalls her doomed affair with Philip Boyes and its tragic aftermath as "a very big mistake," her friend Miss de Vine asks her, "Were you really giving all your mind to it, do you think? Your *mind*? Were you really being as cautious and exacting

---

*Nonetheless, Grevel Lindop refers to her manner in her letters to Williams as "somewhat flirtatious," suggesting a general unfamiliarity with her usual playful style and unwittingly displaying exactly the sort of stereotype a woman like Sayers tended to be up against. See Lindop, *Charles Williams*, 404.

about it as you would be about writing a piece of fine prose?" When Harriet protests that the comparison doesn't seem to make sense, Miss de Vine reminds her that work can bring an "ecstasy" as great as romance in its own way, when one works hard and gets the result just right. And in both work and romance, making hasty and careless decisions is a sign that the subject of your interest "isn't really your subject." Harriet is forced to agree.[14]

Like her own characters, Dorothy learned from bitter experience the peril of letting the heart run away with the mind; she found peace and satisfaction only when she learned to integrate the two. And the place where that happened for her was in her studies and her work.

All of this context is important when considering Sayers's attitudes on gender. As Mary Stewart Van Leeuwen, author of an extensive study on C. S. Lewis and gender issues, has pointed out, Jack's (and Dorothy's) generation grew up at a time when the doctrine of "separate spheres" still held sway.[15] In a nutshell, this doctrine proclaimed that women were worthy of working, even worthy of being in charge, as long as it was the home and children that they were in charge of and they weren't trying to compete with men.

But this doctrine carried very little weight with Dorothy. Fortunate enough to have parents who were great believers in the importance of education for both sexes, and who recognized and nurtured her prodigious gifts—and also to live at a time when women were making tremendous strides in education and the workforce—she believed that women should be as free as men to pursue their God-given callings. Her Christian faith only strengthened and enhanced that belief. In The Mind of the Maker, she argued that when the

Bible says that human beings bear the *imago Dei*, it is saying that we have been made to create, just as God creates (though, of course, on a far more limited scale). When we do good work, we are reflecting the attributes of, and giving glory to, our own Creator.

It must be pointed out that this is not everyone's take on what it means to be made in the image of God. There is a wide variety of theories on what exactly Scripture means by the phrase, encompassing everything from our capacity to have relationships with one another and with God, to our ability to reason, to our special status among all the creatures God made, to our inherent dignity and worth. Sayers's theory on what *imago Dei* means is not among the most commonly accepted, and it does have its flaws; for instance, it doesn't account for those who, through age or infirmity or for some other reason, are unable to work.

But her theory has its strengths as well. Among these is its deliberate implication that women—made in the image of God just like men—are just as capable as men are of doing work of all kinds, including creative work, and that their work ought to be equally encouraged and celebrated as the fruit of a gift and calling from God. It was a point she would stress over and over again in her books and in essays such as "Are Women Human?" in which she wrote, "Once lay down the rule that the job comes first and you throw that job open to every individual, man or woman, fat or thin, tall or short, ugly or beautiful, who is able to do that job better than the rest of the world."[16]

So when Charles Williams shared her love for Dante and encouraged her in studying, writing about, and translating him, he was offering her a precious and rare form of support.

He was recognizing her intellectual strengths and aiding her to do the job she felt called to do. To her mind, there was no greater gift.

The emphasis on the individual here is an important element in Dorothy's thinking on the subject of gender. The same was true for Jack Lewis, who also, more than once, expressed a dislike for generalizations and stereotypes regarding men and women. But there were some key differences between their ideas on the subject.

Separate Spheres

In fact, Jack's views on women—as expressed in his works, his letters, and his behavior toward the women he knew— have provided much fodder for discussion and debate over the years. It's not easy to get a good handle on the topic; as Alan Jacobs expresses it, "The evidence points in several different directions."[17] The fictional men and women in Jack's books, for example, seem to be all over the map. At one moment, a female character might be granted full agency and responsibility; at another, she might be divided from or even subordinated to a male character on what appear to be purely arbitrary grounds. Readers, critics, and scholars are still arguing over the attitudes and actions of Susan and Lucy Pevensie of the Narnia books, Aravis of *The Horse and His Boy*, the Green Lady in *Perelandra*, and more.

Jack was capable, on the one hand, of honoring a female character, like the character of Sarah Smith in *The Great Divorce*, in a way so "radical," as Dr. Joy Jordan-Lake puts it, that it's still appreciated by women everywhere.[18] This inhabitant of heaven is so radiant and full of goodness that the story's narrator actually mistakes her for the Virgin Mary—one of the very highest compliments that any Christian (even a Protestant) could pay. On the other hand, Jack's portrait of Jane Studdock in *That Hideous Strength*, who is portrayed as being clueless about the importance of obedience in marriage and whose career is downplayed, still makes many readers cringe. The question of women's roles and nature in general is one that Jack seems to have struggled with sometimes. He consistently did his best to treat women with honor and respect—many women who knew him have spoken of his kindness to them—and yet his thinking on them was not entirely free from stereotypes and misunderstandings.

The subject of gender in Jack's thinking cannot be addressed without taking into account the fact that he had very little contact with women during his formative years, or indeed well into his adult life. Scholar Alister McGrath goes so far as to say that Lewis "was condemned by history to live and work in an all-male environment."[19] As we have seen, he lost his mother in childhood; though he had other female relatives, at home it was just himself, his father, and his brother, aside from a cook and housemaid. He went to boarding schools for boys, where the majority of the teachers were male; then to a male tutor; then to an all-male college at Oxford. Shortly after that came the army.

Some of these circumstances—especially the mostly male schools and workforce—were shared by most other men of his generation. As a male member of the same generation as Sayers, he was far more influenced by the doctrine of separate spheres than she was. The tragic loss of Jack's mother at such a young age deprived him in those early years of a primary female influence that might have qualified his acceptance of that doctrine. Even though the only role he personally had known her to inhabit was in the home, his mother, as mentioned earlier, was a highly intellectual and well-educated woman. Her death left a gap in his life that would not be filled for quite some time: a distinct lack of such women.

Janie Moore, in addition to being nonreligious, seems to have been nonintellectual as well. Warren Lewis, who disliked her, may have been exaggerating when he claimed never to have seen her reading a book,[20] but she did share very few of Jack's interests, and even fewer after he converted to Christianity. Few of the wives of Jack's friends and colleagues were interested in intellectual pursuits either. While many of the Inklings had good marriages, there was generally a "separate spheres" feel to them.[21] The fact that the Inklings was an all-male club had more to do with Oxford traditions and customs than with any conscious choice by any of its members, but those members seemed quite content with it.

This lack in his life could hardly help shaping some of Jack's opinions of women and their capabilities. He was not enthusiastic when he learned, at the beginning of his teaching career, that many of his pupils would be young women. Van Leeuwen notes that in 1927, he even supported a limit on the number of female students at Oxford.[22]

However, as a good teacher, Jack treated all of his students, male and female, with respect and gave them his best efforts, and it's likely that this contact with female students may have begun to modify his views, possibly without his even realizing it at first. His occasional correspondence with female students, a few of whom kept in touch with him after graduating, was invariably as polite, friendly, and helpful as it was with his male students.

And yet this modification of views would prove to be a slow process. Even as Jack grew in his faith, in some areas he made the all-too-common mistake of reading his cultural views into Scripture, instead of the other way around. As Van Leeuwen suggests, reflecting on the role of mythology in his conversion:

> Lewis seems to have concluded that if more clearly biblical themes such as the "dying yet living God" are foreshadowed in ancient myths, then other mythic themes that he found personally attractive . . . could also come along for the ride.[23]

Both his public and personal writings show that Jack's positions on gender issues—while he sincerely believed them to be Christian positions—often seem to have been based more on his own feelings and inclinations than on rigorous theological argument. His background, upbringing, and limited experience of women, especially academic women, predisposed him to think of them as a sex with whom men—especially academic men—could have little in common. Echoing the old ideas of a separate sphere, he feared the possible implications of a matriarchal form of society because he thought women could not be objective enough about their own families to treat other families fairly.[24]

Moreover, Jack was by nature, as he always freely admitted, a man who gravitated toward hierarchical structures and authority figures. Both his aesthetic side and his philosophical side were drawn to the picture of what he saw as the "dance" of hierarchy, as opposed to the forced "march" that was the drive for equality, which he saw as being too often motivated by pride, envy, and resentment.[25] In a 1945 essay on membership, he explained that he saw the concept of equality as a safeguard of people's rights in a fallen world, not an ideal.

> I do not believe that God created an egalitarian world. I believe the authority of parent over child, husband over wife, learned over simple to have been as much a part of the original plan as the authority of man over beast.[26]

But the presence of sin in the world, Jack went on to say, changed everything:

> The authority of father and husband has been rightly abolished on the legal plane, not because this authority is in itself bad (on the contrary, it is, I hold, divine in origin), but because fathers and husbands are bad.[27]

The wording of that last sentence hints at a fundamental truth that must be remembered about Jack Lewis—in fact, about a sizable portion of humanity. When he was dealing with generalizations he was capable of thinking differently than when he was dealing with individual cases. Indeed, he said as much himself when writing to a correspondent, Margaret Fuller, about a *TIME* magazine cover story about him (which he called "ghastly"). It seems that Fuller had suggested that the profile made him sound misogynistic, for he followed up the comment about its ghastliness with "Who said I disliked women? I never liked or disliked any *generalization*."[28]

While this may very well be true, it's also true that Jack, for much of his life, generally spoke much more sensitively and respectfully to and about women as individuals than as a group. As Van Leeuwen sums it up, "C. S. Lewis was a better man than his theories when it came to women."[29]

This was in large part because, as Dorothy L. Sayers wrote of Lewis to another correspondent in 1954, "I think he has more interior humility than he is apt to be given credit for."[30] Unlike many who shared his firm belief in hierarchy, he didn't hold that belief because he thought he deserved to be at the top of the hierarchy. On the contrary, as he wrote disarmingly in an essay on equality, "I don't deserve a share in governing a hen-roost, much less a nation."[31] That he went on to say that the same is true of most people doesn't take away the impact of the statement; it simply shows that he knew himself to be as fallen as everyone else. Another quote from the essay "Membership" indicates the way he saw his own part in the hierarchical "dance": "It delights me that there should be moments in the services of my own Church when the priest stands and I kneel."[32]

This humility helped to govern his personal relationships with both sexes. Thus, he treated all women with a politeness that verged on the "courtly"—a word that several different people have used to describe his manner in such interactions—and, far more importantly, when he did form a friendship with an intelligent and thoughtful woman, he was willing to listen to her point of view. But these friendships trickled into his life only gradually at first.

So what did these views mean for his friendship with Dorothy L. Sayers?

Transcending Gender

First and foremost, Dorothy fits the clear pattern of female friendship that we see throughout Jack's adult life, once he actually had a chance to start meeting more women. She was a woman of spirit and intellect who spoke straightforwardly with him, even challenging him on some of his most cherished ideas. Almost without exception, this was the kind of woman Jack enjoyed being with most—and, as those familiar with his biography will know, the kind of woman he would eventually marry.

It's ironic, of course, that a man who started out knowing so few intellectual women, and initially being so leery of those he did know, should keep making such friends. And yet these women consistently found his friendship enriching and nourishing, as he did theirs. With friends of intelligence and character, gender could be transcended. And when it was, he was quite ready to put female friends on much the same footing as male friends. Though they may not have been invited to Inklings gatherings, he was willing and even eager to spend time with them, on his own turf and often on theirs as well, if they lived close enough.

With Dorothy, it was mostly on his turf, as he was rarely able to get too far from Oxford (and later Cambridge). We've already seen that he invited her to lunch after those first few exchanges of letters; it was the first of several such invitations and meetings. Neither of them appears to have had the least difficulty with or squeamishness about the prospect, though he was (for most of their friendship) a single man and she a married woman.

For many of us familiar with modern evangelical strictures against men and women dining together, his attitude cannot help but come across as refreshing—and godly. As Aimee Byrd writes, those who surround the practice of eating together with harsh restrictions have forgotten what the act truly signifies for Christians.

When we sit with our brothers and sisters in Christ for a meal, we rehearse for our eternal life in the new heavens and the new earth. Having lunch shouldn't feel like a challenge to marital fidelity. Eating together is a platonic practice intended to bring joy to our friendships.[33]

Though so much of their friendship was conducted by letters, their occasional meetings were not incidental to it; they were crucial for deepening the friendship. Both of them thoroughly enjoyed those meetings and wished they could have met more often.

And Van Leeuwen suggests that the fact that Dorothy was married might actually have made her, in Jack's mind, a "safe" female friend. For a man who had lost his mother so early, had so little comfort in his grief, and then had little contact with women growing up, forming a mature relationship with a woman was not easy, as he himself admitted. Van Leeuwen quotes another of his female friends, Ruth Pitter, as saying, "Losing his mother . . . must have seemed like a black betrayal. If [Jack] was mistrustful of women, it was not hatred, but a burnt child's dread of fire."[34]

Jack was not entirely free of qualms about cross-gender friendships in general—he would go on to write in *The Four Loves* that *philia*, or friendship, between a man and a woman was likely to turn into *eros*, or romantic love, if either found the other attractive.[35] But among women with whom he could talk shop, whose wit and intellect were a match for his own, he seemed to be able to stave off *eros* successfully—with, of course, the one significant exception of Joy Davidman. And, for the record, neither Dorothy nor Jack ever seems to have felt the least bit attracted to each other. Their relationship would stay firmly in the realm of *philia*.

It may very well be that Dorothy too found a level of safety in their friendship. She had been very badly hurt in her youth by her relationships with John Cournos, who had cared little for her needs, desires, and values, and Bill White, who she had hoped might play some role in their child's life but who never did. She had found some comfort in her marriage to Mac Fleming, but as the years went by there was less comfort and more conflict—not the intellectual kind she enjoyed (though Mac was an intelligent man), but more personal and painful conflict. Romance had let her down again and again, but friendship had been a solace, and friendship with a man like Jack in particular must have brought some help and healing with it. Whatever blind spots about women he may have had, and however argumentative he could be, he was a genuinely kind and considerate man.

It also helped, certainly, that both Jack and Dorothy had a true gift for friendship and a great respect for it. Jack's wide-ranging friendships with men, women, and children—including his devotion to the tight-knit circle of the Inklings—are well-known. His chapter on friendship in *The Four Loves* shows just how highly he regarded it. The ancients, he recounted, had held it among the highest of loves, and he argued that they were right to do so. Of good conversations among friends, he wrote, "Life—natural life—has no better gift to give. Who could have deserved it?"[36]

Dorothy, too, was known for being affectionate and generous, and a person who valued friendship highly. As Marjorie Lamp Mead says, "Sayers was a good friend to people."[37] It was true that her personality could be overwhelming; Barbara

Reynolds, who adored her, nevertheless admitted that sometimes she had to spend two days in bed after one of Dorothy's
visits![38] But that was exactly the sort of personality that Jack
enjoyed, in both men and women.

Moreover, the fact that both of them put such a high priority on friendship—cultivating it assiduously and considering
it just as important as other kinds of love—meant that they
had a proper category and role for their interactions. In other
words, they could feel and express friendly affection without
worrying that it was slipping into *eros*. They understood what
friendship meant and were happy simply to be friends.

Also, despite their different ideas about gender, both Dorothy and Jack expressed a distaste for the extremes of femininity and masculinity. When Dorothy, for instance, wrote to
him that she found Pauline Baynes's drawings for his Narnia
books "effeminate,"[39] Jack conceded the point (though he
thought the effeminacy less of a problem than Baynes's "ignorance of animal anatomy") and added: "Don't like either the
ultra feminine or the ultra masculine myself. I prefer *people*."[40]

It's impossible to say whether, when he wrote those words,
Jack could recall what Dorothy had written on the subject
of "the ultra feminine" and "the ultra masculine" in *Gaudy
Night*. (He is said to have had a positively uncanny memory
for passages from books, but it had been a long time since
he had read that one, and as we've seen, he hadn't liked it
when he did.) But whether he recalled it or not, he was, to
an extent, echoing it.

The book is full of reflections on and dialogues about gender; in fact, one particular character's views on what's appropriate for women and what isn't hold the key to the central
mystery. A conversation among several of the characters

about men who put personal relationships before integrity and ethics—and about women who think that this is the right thing to do—leads Lord Peter to observe, "It's odd . . . that the expressions 'manly' and 'womanly' should be almost more offensive than their opposites."[41] He is addressing the common misconception that a truly manly man would put his family above all considerations of honor, and that a truly womanly woman would consider such behavior a great compliment to her; in short, that gender and personal relationships should be the first and foremost dictator of attitudes and behavior. Dorothy was no heavy-handed novelist who weighed down her stories with moralizing, but still, through her characters, she left little doubt of her scorn for that misconception.

This is, of course, a very specific case of gender stereotyping. Jack was speaking rather more broadly when he wrote to Dorothy on the subject. Despite some preconceived notions about male and female tendencies, he truly didn't consider himself a fan of either extreme.

"A Rather Frightened Bachelor"

Both Jack and Dorothy, then, believed that gender was not the most important thing that had to be taken into consideration about a person. And yet it still mattered more to him than it did to her. As much as he made exceptions for individuals, a lot of those generalizations were more deeply ingrained in him than he knew.

This was why, for instance, he could lay so much stress on the difficulties of friendship between the sexes in a book like The Four Loves, even after having enjoyed the friendship of women for much of his adult life. Characteristically, in that book he focused on the problems arising when well-educated men tried to be friends with not-so-well-educated women—and treated it as a generalization, something common to most groups of men and women. Most of his descriptions of ideal friendship had to do with male friendship; he professed such a great ignorance of female friendship that he felt unable to say anything about it. As for male-female friendships, he acknowledged that they could arise when men and women worked in the same profession, but treated them as something rare and difficult to come by.

Of course, having gotten to know him, Dorothy could hardly help but be aware of his attitude—quite possibly more so than he was. In December 1955, she wrote to Barbara Reynolds, who'd had a chance to get acquainted with Lewis when he attended a meeting at her house.

I'm glad you got hold of Lewis. . . . I like him very much, and always find him stimulating and amusing. One just has to accept the fact that there is a complete blank in his mind where women are concerned. Charles Williams and his other married friends used to sit round him at Oxford and tell him so, but there really isn't anything to be done about it. He is not hostile, and he does his best, and actually, for a person with his limitations I think he didn't do too badly with the Lady in *Perelandra*. What he suffers from chiefly, I think, is too much Romantic Literature, far too much Milton, and, as you can see from *Surprised by Joy*, a life bounded by school, the army, and the older universities. . . . He is probably frightened at bottom, like most of these superior males, and, like Milton, is capable of being clumsy and even vulgar—a thing you never find in Dante or Charles Williams, however eccentric or exaggerated their ideas about the sexes.[42]

Regarding Dorothy's use of the word *vulgar*, Dr. Crystal Downing, codirector of the Marion E. Wade Center, suggests, "It seems to me that she invokes it in its original Latin sense of 'common' (as in 'The Vulgate'). So when Milton and Lewis are vulgar about women, they are reflecting the 'common' attitudes of their eras."[43] This is probably much the same definition of the word that Lewis was using when he complained of vulgarity in her essay for the Charles Williams book.

Dorothy was definitely on to something with the comparison between Lewis and Milton. She knew of Jack's love for the poet's works ("I do hope you'll like Milton," he had written in one of his earliest letters to her[44]) and, in fact, had read Jack's book *A Preface to Paradise Lost*—or, as she wrote to Williams, had "coped with" it.[45] While she strove to give Milton the admiration that she realized his greatness deserved—knowing, as she told Williams, that she would "get into trouble with you and Lewis"[46] if she didn't!—she definitely considered him a lesser figure than Dante. What chiefly annoyed her about Milton was the attitude toward women she detected in a passage of Book Four of *Paradise Lost*, which describes Adam and Eve:

> For contemplation he and valour formed;
> For softness she and sweet attractive grace;
> He for God only, she for God in him.[47]

That last line, putting the sexes on an unequal footing before God, violently offended not only Dorothy's ideas about the rights and responsibilities of women but also her theology. She often quoted it throughout her writings as a sort of short-hand description of anyone who was clueless about women and relationships. Back in 1930, for instance, she had thrown a cheeky reference to the passage into *Strong Poison*, when Harriet and Peter are discussing her late lover, Philip Boyes. Though Philip had seemed the embodiment of an enlightened modern poet, it transpires that his idea of romance had been all about wanting a woman's subservient "devotion," never her friendship. "Such a Victorian attitude . . . for a man with advanced ideas," observes Peter dryly. "He for God only, she for God in him, and so on."[48]

Dorothy would keep pulling out the phrase whenever she caught wind of such "Victorian attitudes" in men she knew or read; to her mind, it summed up those attitudes so perfectly. And, yes, she would apply it to Lewis, too, in a letter to Barbara Reynolds.[49] (Though she knew Williams was an admirer of Milton as well, it doesn't seem to have occurred to her to apply the comparison to him. As we'll see, perhaps she should have.)

But there may have been more to it than that. Dorothy did tend to be excessively harsh with Jack sometimes for even bringing up the subject of sexuality, gender, or marriage. When he had used the comparison about love and marriage in his letter (cited in ch. 3) about the "itch" to write certain things, she had replied a little frostily, "I do not care much for these sexual analogies of yours."[50] And yet she had gone on to use a far more explicit sexual analogy in her next letter to him. Referring to his feeling that "A doctrine never seems dimmer to me than when I have just successfully defended it,"[51] she whimsically suggested that the problem might be

"You are tired. Having united yourself with the doctrine—you hope fruitfully—you are worried by its plaintive cry: 'But do you still love me?' Reassure it courteously, and go to sleep."[52]

Perhaps it wasn't so much the mention of love and marriage that bothered Sayers but the question of whether, as an unmarried man, Lewis had the right to say anything on the subject at all. Despite all she had said about the reasons for the "complete blank" in his view of women, at bottom she suspected that the real trouble was that he was "a rather frightened bachelor." And thus, she wrote to another correspondent, he was "apt to write shocking nonsense about women and marriage."[53]

What's interesting here is that Dorothy generally vigorously opposed what she and Jack both referred to as the "personal heresy," or what is also known as the biographical fallacy—that is, basing one's opinion of an author's work on his personal history. But because Jack was a friend, not just another writer, she may have felt freer to examine and dissect his limitations and their bearing on his work. And she may have had a point; as we'll see later, both she and Jack seem to have thought that he gained greater wisdom about women and marriage in some ways after he himself got married.

But she may also have unwittingly let his lack of experience at this time prejudice her against anything he had to say on the subject. Some of her writings—from her letters to John Cournos to her reflections on Dante's superiority to Milton—show something of a tendency on her part to consider marriage a higher state than singleness, and sexually experienced people more mature in some ways than the inexperienced. At the very least, she thought they had a better chance at understanding the opposite sex and bringing a balanced, broadminded point of view to relations between the sexes.

"You see, I *know* now," she had written to Cournos in 1923, after her son's birth, "what I was only sure of before, that the difference between the fruitful and the barren body is just that between conscious health and unconscious—what shall I call it?—uneasiness, discomfort, something that isn't quite health. . . . The fact is, I'm afraid, that I'm the person you are always talking about and don't like when you meet her—a really rather primitive woman."[54] It may have been a natural feeling, especially for a woman who had just given birth. But—just like some of those beliefs of Jack's about gender that she would one day deplore—this feeling, too, was somewhat at odds with the Christian faith she professed, which holds both celibacy and family life in equal esteem.

With other audiences, and with increasing maturity, she would express her feelings on the subject with a little more restraint. And characteristically for her, she did on some level have an awareness of her weakness. She even brought it into *Gaudy Night*, where she had Harriet, while surrounded by single women at Oxford (at a time when single women were expected to be chaste), wrestle with a similar prejudice against the state of lifelong celibacy and barrenness and come to realize just how stereotypical, unfair, and wrong that prejudice was. (Especially when—spoiler alert—the criminal in the story is unmasked and turns out to be a widow and mother!) But Dorothy's feelings may have lingered subconsciously and colored her perception of anything Jack had to say on the subject.

That doesn't mean she was entirely wrong about Jack's attitude toward women. And she did what she could to help lead him to a better understanding of masculinity and femininity in general. For instance, when he praised her style of translation as "masculine," acknowledging that he understood many women didn't particularly care for the label, she wrote back:

> No—I don't mind a style being called "masculine," provided that its pejorative opposite is understood to be, not "feminine" but "effeminate." The trouble is that "feminine" is used, critically, in both a good and a bad sense. There is a positive and good feminine quality—Jane Austen, I suppose, is the supreme exponent—a style like a cat's paw, all velvet and sinews and still points—which male writers achieve only with difficulty or not at all. . . . But there is also a bad femininity, which consists of female sensibility in the wrong place— "flowers on the work-bench." There is, in the same way, a bad masculinity, which comes out in things like Dickens's virtuous heroines, who are only projections of the male yearnings— the counterpoint of the "maiden's prayer" kind of hero. The bad masculinity and the bad femininity are, perhaps, two different kinds of sentimentality. . . . But the whole terminology of the subject needs overhauling.[55]

Jack's future wife, Joy, would one day pick up where Dorothy left off in the instructional process. Lewis records in his book A Grief Observed, written after Joy's death, that once when he had praised Joy for her "masculine virtues," "she soon put a stop to that by asking me how I'd like to be praised for my feminine ones."[56] Jack acknowledged the wit and profundity of the remark, but maintained that he had found in Joy both the masculine and the feminine qualities he liked best. Even if he had not fully comprehended all that Dorothy had tried to show him, something in him had absorbed the idea that it was possible and even desirable for a person of either gender to encompass the best of both worlds.

Misreading Williams

But it was possible for both Jack and Dorothy to get things very wrong about some male-female relationships. That passage in her December 1955 letter to Barbara Reynolds describing Inklings meetings (where the other men supposedly gave Jack an occasional talking-to about his views on women), besides giving us an interesting view of Jack through Dorothy's eyes, brings us back to Charles Williams, and his influence on and friendships with both Dorothy and Jack. It helps to show us why she had found Williams such a valuable guide. And yet anyone remotely familiar with Williams's biography will recognize a deep irony in the passage.

The truth is, there were aspects of Williams's life that neither Dorothy nor Jack knew about—aspects that call into serious question the high view of womanhood that Dorothy blithely ascribed to him, not to mention his right to tell off anyone on the subject as she pictures him doing. It was very likely Williams himself who provided her with this picture; he was the only Inkling, besides Jack himself, who was a friend of hers. The picture was probably not completely inaccurate; we know from other sources that Jack's male friends sometimes took him to task for his attitudes toward women. But it was not completely accurate either.

(Jack, incidentally, portrayed those gatherings rather differently when he wrote to Williams's widow shortly after her husband's death, "Whenever Charles disagreed with anything we had said about women in general, it was a common turn of raillery to reply, 'Oh Charles!—of course he's in love, so his opinions on that subject are worthless!'"[57])

As a matter of fact, Williams's ideas about the sexes—indeed, his ideas in general—were far more "eccentric," to borrow Dorothy's word, than either she or Jack ever dreamed. Despite his Anglican faith, he was also fascinated by the occult and belonged to a group that experimented with magical practices, though with a veneer of Christianity. Moreover, he used his undisputed power over people to make "disciples" of various young women. Throughout his adult life, including during his marriage, he engaged in a series of intense emotional affairs with these women, which were generally technically chaste but involved his ordering them around, emotionally abusing them, and even indulging in "semi-sexual, semi-magical rituals," like spanking them with a sword.[58]

What his more orthodox Christian friends would have thought of such practices can easily be imagined. They likely would have been all the more startled because so many of them, Dorothy and Jack included, had placed him on such a high pedestal. Jack had watched him lecture Oxford undergraduates on chastity, in the context of Milton's poem *Comus*, so beautifully and fervently that he was left marveling, "I have at last, if only for once, seen a university doing what it was founded to do: teaching Wisdom."[59] Jack and Tolkien themselves had helped to arrange the lecture series. (Tolkien liked Williams, but with reservations—even at the time, according to R. E. "Humphrey" Havard, Tolkien found Williams's writing a little too inclined toward the occult. He was troubled by things like the important role played by a deck of tarot cards in Williams's novel *The Greater Trumps*.[60] As Philip and Carol Zaleski put it in their book *The Fellowship*:

The Literary Lives of the Inklings, Tolkien "may have suspected [correctly] that behind these plot devices lay personal occult experience."[61])

To be sure, Jack probably would have understood Williams's sexual temptations better than most, having indulged in his own sadomasochistic fantasies in his younger days. But Christianity had made a great difference to Jack's sexual ideas and attitudes. For Williams, this does not seem to have been the case. Whether this has anything to do with the fact that Williams was a cradle Christian, while Jack came to genuine faith later in life, is hard to say. Dorothy L. Sayers, a fellow cradle Christian, believed that sort of thing did make a great difference in a number of ways. She once wrote of Jack that "he has experienced a genuine religious conversion, which is more than most of us have, and is always a little frightening in its effects because of the way it alters values."[62]

Having come to Christ and then, as a consequence, accepted church teachings on sexuality, Jack was able to look back on a clean break between his old sexual values and his new ones, and to identify the old ones firmly with his pre-Christian period, a time that was past. Williams, on the other hand, seems to have allowed Christianity and occultism and sadomasochism all to grow up together in his thinking until he could no longer tell where one ended and another began—a state of mind that, ultimately, was decidedly more frightening in its effects.

At any rate, when faint rumors of what had been going on did reach their ears, Jack and Dorothy found it all but impossible to believe that the friend who had seemed so saintly could have deliberately been involved in anything of the sort. Jack did know that Williams had a following of devoted young women. He could hardly help knowing; it was obvious to anyone who saw as much of him as Jack and the other Inklings did. But it appears that Williams claimed he was innocent of taking any initiative or doing anything wrong in these relationships, and Lewis believed him.

The extent of that belief can be seen in Jack's reply to an unknown correspondent who wrote to ask for advice about how to handle a young woman who was too devoted to him:

> I wish Charles Williams were alive: this was just his pigeon. His solution was, in a peculiar way, to teach 'em the *ars amandi* [art of love]* and then bestow them on other (younger) men. *Sic vos non vobis* [for you, but not yours]. He was not only a lover himself but the cause that love was in other men.[63]

Just as with Dorothy's idea of how Jack's married male friends had talked to him about women, one can only suppose that this was the spin that Williams himself had put on the matter when he talked to Jack about it.

Likewise, Dorothy wrote in 1950 to a correspondent who was doing research on Williams that "he attracted to himself (by no fault of his own) a good deal of rather indiscriminating admiration, and one finds in some quarters a tendency to erect him into the object of an esoteric cult."[64] But just a few years later, in a 1954 letter, she had progressed to the point of admitting, "He was prompted, I am sure, by his generous love for people; but he did not quite escape permitting a cult

---

*The phrase *ars amandi* originally referred to sexual love, but given the context of the conversation and Lewis's own moral convictions—not to mention his belief that Charles and Michal Williams had had an ideal marriage—it seems likely that Lewis meant to argue that Williams was practicing *agape* or *philia*, rather than *eros*.

of himself." Yet she added quickly, "But I hate finding weaknesses in Charles, who showed me so much."[65] And in an undated letter, she insisted that he had been firmly opposed to the actual practice of magic.[66]

But the signs of something wrong were there, if Williams's friends had been able to interpret them. In that same year of 1954, Dorothy and Jack found themselves exchanging mildly anxious letters about Williams's widow, Michal, and son, Michael, with whom they had both kept in touch on and off. Both could sense a problem in the family that Williams had left behind. "She is a good deal of an invalid," Dorothy wrote of Michal Williams, "and she is full of queer, rambling grievances—some, I think, partly justified, others no doubt exaggerated. I find her company very exhausting, though mercifully she likes me and is pathetically grateful for any kindness. I think she has genuinely suffered a good deal from persons claiming to be Charles's spiritual wives, and from the Household of Taliessin generally," by which she seems to have meant the spiritual community with which Williams had surrounded himself.[67] (*Taliessin through Logres* was the title of one of Williams's Arthurian poetry cycles.)

She worried, too, that Michal's gloom was having a bad effect on her adult son, Michael, who lived with her and who was emotionally unstable and struggling to establish himself. Living with his mother must be, Dorothy thought, "like living with a quiet, melancholy vampire."[68] Jack, who had recently had the young man over to dinner, agreed that Michael seemed to be "over-mothered."[69]

On the contrary, according to what we now know of the family life of the Williamses, Michael's mother seems to have been the least of his problems. "Under-fathered" might have been more like it, at least during the young man's early years (to Charles Williams's credit, he had tried hard to be a better father as his son reached young adulthood). Both Jack and Dorothy had fallen into the trap of thinking that any problem with the son must be attributed to the mother, when in fact it was the mother who had borne far more than her share of the parenting.

But Dorothy would never know the full extent of Williams's "weaknesses"; she died before some of his "disciples" began to write publicly about them. His wife and son, however burdened by the fallout from those weaknesses, seem to have kept the bulk of it private. Whether Jack read any of the later revelations about him, we cannot know for sure. If he did, he left no record of reading them or of his reaction to them.

Looking back from our vantage point, we can find it easy to fault Jack, Dorothy, and Williams's other friends for idolizing him as they did and for having such a hard time believing ill of him. But it has to be remembered that, for one thing, they all lived in a very different time. That may sound like a cliché, but after all, clichés become clichés for a reason. The simple truth is that Charles Williams lived during a period when it was easier, even for other women, to discount women's accounts of their own experiences. Besides this, many of the women who had surrounded Williams seemed to remain more or less in his thrall and were still saying good things about him after his death despite the less savory aspects of his behavior. For instance, Joan Wallis, a disciple whom he had coerced to "submit to his personal [spanking] rituals" because he believed they helped him release his creativity, nonetheless called him "the most remarkable and good man I've ever met."[70]

That comment is just one more demonstration that Williams's personality and effect on other people were something truly out of the ordinary. Those like Wallis, who hated what he did to them, still felt loyal to him; those who were unaware of those secret activities thought him next door to a saint. It wasn't just the Inklings and Dorothy L. Sayers who felt it. Philip and Carol Zaleski quote T. S. Eliot as saying, "I have never known a healthier-minded man than Williams," and W. H. Auden as saying that, when he met Williams, "For the first time in my life [I] felt myself in the presence of personal sanctity."[71]

This effect is all the stranger when one reads about Williams's true thoughts and feelings about other people. The Zaleskis note with great insight that Williams actually felt "an inability to be at ease with either sex. Men he must impress, women he must teach or rule." They trace a pattern of "anger and resentment" in his letters, quoting passages like "'I dislike people, & I hate being with them'; 'You can't imagine how I dislike people's *faces*'; 'There are wells of hate in one which are terrifying.'"[72] Of course, there are many people who feel such feelings but strive to overcome them. But in Williams's case, it seems more accurate to say that he managed to keep from expressing them straightforwardly, yet allowed them to emerge in strange, distorted forms.

A Friendship of Equals

Jack's and Dorothy's own personalities have to be taken into account here as well. Jack was always eager for friends who shared both his spiritual and intellectual interests. He famously defined friendship as a relationship "born . . . at the moment when one man says to another, 'What! You too? I thought that no one but myself . . .'"[73] And in fact, he and Williams had first become acquainted when they wrote fan letters to each other at the same time about each other's books (Williams's *The Place of the Lion* and Jack's *The Allegory of Love*, which Williams had received at Oxford University Press to do some marketing work on and had ended up titling). The joy of friendship with someone whose mind and sensibilities were so in tune with his own, in so many ways, may have blinded Jack to any red flags about Williams's character or behavior, even if Williams had not so carefully hidden his private life from the Inklings.

As for Dorothy, Marjorie Lamp Mead observes that she never lost her love of the dramatic or her flair for playing a role, and her hero-worship of Williams may have been just one more example of that. Of course, her liking for him and his work was perfectly genuine, as was her great appreciation of his insights on Dante. But in her case, the high pedestal may have been, at least to some extent, simply a delightful game.[74]

At different times, without their knowledge, both Jack and Dorothy were referred to as "disciples" of Williams. Many years after Dorothy's death, Williams's friend Anne Spalding rather disparagingly recalled Dorothy's first visit to him:

When she arrived, she was very much the successful author, lecturing C. W. on how he ought to get his books into mass circulation by doing this and that with publishers and agents. Twenty-four hours later she was his disciple, sitting at his feet.[75]

It was Williams himself who, aware of his increasing influence on Jack's thinking and writing, told a friend, "Lewis is becoming a mere disciple."[76] What bothered him about this was that, as Jack was so much more famous than he was, Williams might be seen as taking ideas from Jack instead of the other way around!

But the truth is, they never were his disciples, not in the way that Williams and his private circle formally used the word. Neither of them was cut out to be the "disciple" of a fellow human being. Dazzled as they may have been by his work and his charisma, and blinded as they may have been to what was going on with him behind the scenes, both of them had too much maturity, sense, and strength of character for that. Dorothy had long since outgrown the stage of true hero-worship, and anyway, both she and Jack—as committed Christians who considered the occult dangerous and anti-Christian—doubtless would have considered such "discipleship" blasphemy. Besides that, Dorothy was very much the dominant figure in her relationship with Williams, something he never could have stood for in a "disciple," especially a female one.

It's hard to imagine that Dorothy would not have been troubled by Williams's exploitation and manipulation of vulnerable young women. But he had made her believe that his views on women were very much like her own, and she had seen in his thinking and writing what she wanted to see—much as Jack had heard in Williams's Milton lectures what he wanted to hear. It's impossible to say whether that would have changed if Williams had lived longer—if Dorothy would have found out the truth and what she would have made of it (or if Jack would have either, for that matter). Although she consistently spoke against the "personal heresy," knowing about Williams's real views and practices may have given his work a different color for her.

But in any event, it was Jack Lewis, after all—notwithstanding the "complete blank" Dorothy had detected in his mind—who proved to be the better friend for a woman of her intelligence and strength.

While Tolkien may have been turned off by her ideas and Williams by her personality, Jack freely admitted to being challenged and stimulated by both—and liking the experience. His views on women as a whole, however theologically unsupported or even occasionally backward they might be, did not prevent him from treating an individual woman with courtesy and esteem, from thinking of her as a true colleague and compatriot, or from learning from her. He did not have to "rule," dominate, or put down a woman. And if he had once held back from arguing with Dorothy out of courtesy, he now genuinely recognized and respected her insights; he could critique her work and her thinking, but always as an equal. Unlike the fictional Philip Boyes or the real Charles Williams, Jack Lewis was capable of true friendship with a woman.

In turn, Dorothy was a valuable figure in his life, helping to clear away some of his faulty thinking and showing him just what an intelligent and spirited woman was capable of. In the letters Jack wrote to her, we can trace a slow development in his thinking, a tendency to start looking back and questioning things he had never really noticed or had taken for granted. In 1955, he wrote in response to a letter of hers that appears to have been lost: "I hadn't really thought about it before, but of course Tolkien's females are as you describe them." The editor's footnote in the collected letters tells us (alas!) that "it is not known how Sayers described them."[77] Yet his response shows his respect for her opinion. With her guidance, he could consider this aspect of a book he knew and loved so well in a new light.

Also in 1955, in an exchange of letters after Dorothy reviewed his book *Surprised by Joy*, Jack told her he was glad she liked the way he had portrayed his father (she seems to have been one of the few who did like it), and went on to add:

> I had dimly realized that the old-fashioned way (my Father did it exquisitely) of talking to all young women was v. like an adult way of talking to small boys. It explains not only why some women grew up vapid but also why others grew up almost (if we may coin the word) *viricidal* [wanting to kill men].[78]

Dorothy picked up the term, and the train of thought, in her reply:

> Worse than vapidity or viricidal (lovely word!) tendencies was the fundamental dishonesty involved—on the one side habitual concealment, and the proceeding to every objective by an elaborate strategy; on the other, a perverse male satisfaction in being wheedled and "managed" . . . a mutual complacent contempt which was scarcely good for either party.[79]

While the two of them might never have quite seen fully eye to eye on some of these issues, their friendship was built on a foundation of honesty, humility, and a willingness to listen, which safeguarded it from contempt and helped both friends to grow in empathy and understanding.

Five

"Sister Dinosaur"

In June 1947, at the end of a letter to Jack about his book *Miracles* and her translation of the *Inferno*, Dorothy wrote:

> I have no news, except that—looking forward to the confidently-expected food crisis, I have purchased two Hens. In their habits they display, respectively Sense and Sensibility, and I have therefore named them Elinor and Marianne. Elinor is a round, comfortable, motherly-looking little body, who lays one steady, regular, undistinguished egg per day. . . . Marianne is leggier, timid, and liable to hysterics. . . . On the days when she lays no egg she nevertheless goes and sits in the nest for the usual time, and seems to imagine that nothing more is required. As my gardener says: "She just *thinks* she's laid an egg". Too much imagination—in fact, Sensibility. But when she does lay an egg it is larger than Elinor's. But you cannot wish to listen to this cackle.[1]

In fact, Lewis was delighted by the anecdote, responding, "I loved hearing about Elinor and Marianne. You are a real letter-writer. I am not."[2]

"Noble and Joyous Things"

The hens marked a turning point. This is the first letter we have between the two of them in which Dorothy recounted a personal anecdote or wrote anything at all that wasn't related to theology, literature, culture, or work in general. Which is not to say that theirs had not been a real friendship before this point. Friendship, for both of them, was built on just such common interests and enthusiasms; it had to begin with these if it was to become true friendship. No other kind of friendship appealed to them more than that built on the life of the mind.

And yet, if it lasted long enough, even intellectual friendship was bound to go broader and deeper, to begin to incorporate all areas of life. David J. Theroux, founder of the C. S. Lewis Society of California, quotes Lewis as saying, "Friendship must be about something," and yet goes on to add, "For Lewis, though, friendship in its essence was much more than the pursuit of common interests—it was a selfless and joyous harmony among equals."[3] And Jack himself wrote in *The Four Loves*, "All who share [a common interest] will be our companions; but one or two or three who share something more will be our Friends."[4] True and lasting friendship must begin with common interests, but ultimately it must transcend them.

Thus, the years that followed would see Jack's and Dorothy's communications, even as they kept their main focus on the intellectual realm, become more personal, informal, chatty—in a word, friendlier. He continued to express great pleasure in receiving and reading her letters, which says something important about them. For Jack Lewis, the reading and writing of letters, which he did conscientiously for hours every day, could be a very weary business, given the amount and types of correspondence he received. But he consistently referred to Dorothy's letters as something special—the kind of letters he truly enjoyed reading and responding to, not the kind that were merely a duty.

Almost from the beginning, he adopted a tone with her that was more playful and lighthearted than that which he used with many other new correspondents. Later, he closed one letter to her by saying that he had "thousands of letters from mere acquaintances to deal with," suggesting that hers were something quite different.[5] In another letter, which he was forced to shorten for lack of time, he lamented, "Oh the mails: every bore in two continents seems to think I *like* getting letters. One's real friends are precisely the people one never gets time to write to."[6] And as we've seen, more than once he insisted that she was a better letter writer than he was.

It wasn't just her letters that he enjoyed but her company as well. Again and again he expressed a desire for more of it, ending his letters with thoughts like "I wish we met sometimes"; "It is long since we met"; "I . . . wish you sometimes came to Oxford"; and "I do hope we can meet in the summer."[7] Dorothy, too, seemed to look forward to and enjoy their meetings: "I do hope . . . that we can meet and have a good talk. It is a long time since we set eyes on each other, though we have kept in touch by hand o'write."[8]

For nonacademics—perhaps for modern audiences in general—it can seem almost comical at times to see just how much the two of them prioritized professional and intellectual matters even in conversations that were ostensibly about personal matters. For instance, most of Dorothy's letters continued to start off with reflections on Dante, regardless of their main topic! But at the same time, they seemed to stimulate a well of creativity in each other that took a variety of forms. They would send each other poems they had written (or ask for help with poems in the process of being written); share amusing anecdotes; talk about what they had been reading for pleasure, not just for work; and send Christmas cards. Dorothy had developed a habit of sending out elaborate homemade ones, often containing original narratives written by herself and artwork by professional artists, and she always made sure to include Jack on her Christmas list. "You are always producing noble and joyous things," he wrote to her admiringly after receiving one such project. He particularly liked a card with lots of little doors in it, but struggled to get all of the little doors open![9]

In 1954, after he accepted the chair of Medieval and Renaissance Literature at Cambridge University, Dorothy sent a card designed just for him, with what Barbara Reynolds calls "an allegorical drawing."[10] The allegory was apparently so difficult to decipher that Jack responded with a poem beginning, "Dear Dorothy, I'm puzzling hard / What underlies your cryptic card."[11] She immediately dashed off and sent back a poem of her own to explain the meaning (something about the spirit of Genius guiding him to revive learning), ending it: "*Allegoria explicit.* / A puzzle framed so neat and fit

/ Should not have proved 'more hard to guess / Than sphinx or Themis.' —D. L. S."[12]

Their conversation—much like the dialogue Dorothy wrote for Lord Peter Wimsey—was saturated with literary allusions, regardless of what they happened to be discussing. "Your letter shines amid the day's mail like a good deed in a naughty world," Jack once wrote to her, borrowing a phrase from Shakespeare's *The Merchant of Venice*.[13] When the University of St. Andrews awarded Jack an honorary doctorate, Dorothy teasingly opened her next letter: "Dear Mr, I should say Dr Lewis, but the other comes so natural," a paraphrase of the cringingly humble Uriah Heep in Dickens's *David Copperfield*.[14] (Dorothy herself would receive an honorary doctorate in 1950 from the University of Durham, in recognition of her translation of Dante's *Inferno*.)

In fact, in that more formal era, the issue of names, even between friends, was a complex one. It was fully twelve years before the two of them got around to calling each other by their first names, and that happened only because of that change in position for Jack. After she had written to congratulate him on the new position at Cambridge, and apparently asked what he should now be called, he pointed out, "If you wd. call me Jack as others do, the difficulty wd. not arise. (I believe such suggestions ought to come from the lady, but years pass and the lady doesn't move!)"[15] From then on they were "Dorothy" and "Jack" to each other.

At the same time these shifts in tone were taking place, larger and deeper shifts were taking place in the background. Both of their lives were changing significantly in the late 1940s and early 1950s, as was the culture around them. As other relationships formed, ended, and altered, this particular friendship offered some comforting familiarity and stability to both.

Inklings Eroding

Jack still had his core group of friends and critics, the Inklings, but sadly, by the late 1940s the group was no longer what it had been. Meetings were less regular, and, when they did take place, less free and open than before. Colin Duriez, author of *Tolkien and C. S. Lewis: The Gift of Friendship*, pinpoints an evening in October 1949, when none of them came to Lewis's rooms for the usual meeting, as "the end of the Inklings as a reading group, even though the friends continued to meet informally . . . until the year of Lewis's death."[16]

More than one reason has been suggested for this. Some have speculated that Charles Williams's charismatic presence had thrown the group off balance, captivating Jack to an extent that made Tolkien feel left out, and that equilibrium was never restored even after Williams's death. But looking at the group's interactions at the time, this does not seem to have been the case. Tolkien and Williams got along well at the time, even though Tolkien never truly fell under his influence as Jack did and thought Jack perhaps a little too susceptible to that influence. It was only much later, after Tolkien read some of the writings of Williams's "disciples," that he truly started to distance himself from Williams's life and legacy, stating that the two of them had liked each other but "had nothing to say to one another at deeper (or higher) levels."[17] But in any case, jealousy—unless Tolkien felt it secretly and hid it carefully—does not seem to have been a serious factor in their relationship.

It seems more likely, based on the evidence we have, that the increasing sharpness of the criticism within the circle was what ultimately undermined it. Certainly criticism had always been allowed, even encouraged; as Jack wrote to Williams when critiquing some of the latter's poems early in their correspondence, even before Williams joined the group, "I embrace the opportunity of establishing the precedent of brutal frankness, without which our acquaintance . . . would easily be a mere butter bath!"[18]

Yet at the same time, the Inklings had come to depend strongly on each other for support, and when that support was withheld, the wounds often went deep. Tolkien was hurt by Hugo Dyson's abrasive remarks about *The Lord of the Rings*, to the point where he felt uncomfortable reading to the group, despite Jack's ongoing encouragement. "Eventually," according to the Zaleskis, "Dyson bullied his way into the censor's seat and managed to ban all readings of *Lord* while he was present."[19]

But Tolkien was not only a recipient of painful criticism; he could dish it out as well. Jack himself would later be deeply affected by Tolkien's dislike of his Narnia books, and possibly also by Tolkien's disapproval of his popular works of theology. At times, Tolkien's opinions on his work seem to have undermined Jack's confidence in it.[20]

Meanwhile, Owen Barfield, one of Jack's other closest friends, was nevertheless nursing a longstanding grievance against Jack. Many years previously, after a lengthy period of debate and discussion with Lewis over Barfield's pet philosophy, anthroposophy (which they called their "Great War"), Lewis had ended by simply refusing to discuss the subject anymore, and he stuck to it.[21] He gave full credit to Barfield's anthroposophical arguments for helping lead to his own conversion to Christianity,[22] but the subject and the argument had begun to distress him too much to go on with it. Barfield remained passionately devoted to anthroposophy but felt lonely and misunderstood because his friends, along with his wife, Maud, wanted nothing to do with it.

At any rate, as the cracks in the Inklings widened and deepened, Jack increasingly found himself in need of other friends to turn to for discussion and critique, including Sayers. Dorothy, as we have seen, could be as sharply critical as any of his other friends, but with a fundamental difference: at bottom, she respected and appreciated the main body of his work. He could discuss with her both his apologetics work and his fiction, and be assured of a largely sympathetic (if not always concurring) listener. This is not to say that his friendship with Dorothy replaced any of his other friendships; he would remain friends with Tolkien, Barfield, and most of the others until the end of his life. But she helped to fill a need that had emerged as the solidarity and support of the group had eroded. And she could be a staunch defender in public as well as an appreciative listener in private.

In July 1955, for instance, Jack happened across a letter to the editor of the *Spectator* that Dorothy had written, vigorously defending the Narnia books against a critic who had not only disliked but grossly misunderstood them. It turned out that, without Jack having been aware of it, Dorothy knew the series quite well. She wrote about her liking for it in a 1956 letter to Barbara Reynolds, who was reading them with her young daughter. Dorothy expressed in particular her appreciation that

the girls, on the whole, are given as much courage as the
boys, and more virtue . . . and they are even allowed to fight
with bows and arrows, though not with swords—a curious
sex-distinction which I don't quite approve of; as though to
kill at a distance were more feminine than to kill at close
quarters![23]

But that minor point aside, her impression of Narnia had
been decidedly positive. So in her letter to the *Spectator*, in
her own inimitably blunt fashion, she set the critic straight
about both Jack's theology (the critic having mistaken Aslan
for an archangel rather than a Christ figure) and the rules of
fantasy, which she argued were much more lenient than the
critic allowed.

Jack was touchingly surprised to find that Dorothy had
been reading his "opuscules" (little works) and grateful to
her for standing up for him against the "nit-wit."[24] Her words
about his books in that article—including her assertion that
"Professor Lewis's theology and pneumatology are as accurate
and logical here as in his other writings"—must have helped
to soothe the old sting of Tolkien's disapproval.[25]

From then on Jack and Dorothy discussed Narnia freely
(including Dorothy's dislike of Pauline Baynes's illustrations,
referred to earlier), and she confessed herself as eager as any
child for the publication of *The Last Battle*.[26] He made sure
to send her a copy as soon as it came out.

"Yours Is the Very Nicest"

Dorothy was, of course, immersed in her own major work at
this period. Her translation of the *Inferno*, the first volume

of Dante's *Divine Comedy*, appeared in 1949, and throughout the early 1950s she was busy on the second volume, the *Purgatorio*.

It's doubtful that Dorothy felt as deeply in need of support in her endeavors as Jack did at this time. She effectively created her own support, chattering excitedly and at great length about Dante to any of her friends who would listen, regardless of their own level of interest and expertise. But she of course continued to feel the loss of Charles Williams, just as she was embarking on the project, as a major blow. She had counted on his knowledge, insight, and advice. And of course, as patient and encouraging as her circle generally was, it was easier to have helpful and substantive discussions with friends who already knew and appreciated the poet and his work. Fortunately, she did have her friend Barbara Reynolds, who was a Dante scholar (and who would one day finish Dorothy's translation of the third volume, the *Paradiso*, after Dorothy's death).

She also had Jack Lewis. Along with Reynolds, he helped to fill the gap Williams had left. He could be depended on for friendly argument—which she so often found stimulating—about her methods and interpretation, as well as for encouragement and appreciation of her efforts. He expressed astonished admiration for all the hard work she was putting into her translation. He held a party for her at Oxford in 1949 when she went there to give a lecture on Dante for the Summer School of Italian Studies.[27] And he sent her two glowing letters about her translation of *The Inferno*, one while he was still reading it and one after he had finished. That is, they were glowing by his and her standards. Typically—and as she would certainly have expected by now—he tempered his praise with a critique of her style.

> The colloquialisms will be the largest of all hostile criticism.
> That you are no doubt prepared for. I approve a great many
> of them: just now & then, however, I feel they suggest not
> intimacy & directness but flippancy. . . . But . . . every live
> rendering must sacrifice some things to achieve others. You
> have chosen to get in Dante the lively "scientifictionist"
> [science fiction writer] at all (reasonable) costs, and as all
> your predecessors chose to get in the *altissimo poeta* [the most
> exalted of poets] at *all* costs, this was the right thing to do.
> It is a strong, exciting, view of Dante from one particular
> angle, and that is worth any number of timid, safe versions.
> Your version of any passage will always be *one* of the things
> I shall take into account in trying to understand any dif-
> ficult place: and that, which those who haven't thought on
> the matter, wd. take for faint praise, is, as you know, saying
> a lot.[28]

This, as Jack well knew—they had discussed the matter frequently while she was working on her translation—was exactly the kind of thing she felt strongly about and hungered to discuss. "I've had a lot of nice letters about the *Inferno*," Dorothy replied, "but I think yours is the very nicest, because you understood so well what the thing's all about, and what a translation aims at."[29] They would continue to go back and forth about both content and style, including what consti-tuted "flippancy" and how colloquial was too colloquial, but she knew that in him she was assured of an understanding, supportive, and deeply engaged reader—one who assured her he would "fight to the death" for her "lighter & freer view of

D[ante]" even while enthusiastically and endlessly arguing with her over the nuances of it.[30]

Perhaps Jack's own experience popularizing subjects like theology, to the dismay of many of his colleagues and even his close friends, gave him more sympathy for what Dorothy was trying to do with Dante. And popularize Dante she did. Her translation was a great success, and, as she heard from many readers, did exactly what she hoped it would do: revitalized a poet who had for too long, through no fault of his own, been regarded as dry, dusty, and dull. "Since Dorothy L. Sayers," wrote Ian Thomson in 1994, "Dante has had more English-speaking readers in the last 40 years than the preceding six and a quarter centuries. Trimmed of the Victorian distortions, Dante is a rousing read."[31]

Loss and Freedom

As always, though, professional preoccupations came accompanied by personal ones. On that front, Jack and Dorothy had another experience in common in the early 1950s: each lost someone who had been central to his or her life for many years. And oddly enough, for each of them, the loss was not as devastating as might be expected.

Dorothy had striven faithfully, even as her career took up more and more of her time, to give top priority to her marriage to Mac. It had grown ever more difficult as the years went on and his illnesses grew worse, along with his addiction to alcohol. His doctors had trouble diagnosing exactly what the problems were, as all kinds of symptoms were involved, from stomach trouble to sciatica to high blood pressure to neuritis, but they were believed to have stemmed mostly from his war service. In Mac's last few years he was depressed, jealous of his wife's success, and frequently an invalid, needing so much care that Dorothy could rarely leave home for more than a couple of nights at a time. She turned down multiple engagements and increasingly put aside her work—even though they needed her earnings—to tend to him.

Mac died of a cerebral hemorrhage on June 9, 1950, at the age of sixty-eight, just four days before Dorothy's fifty-seventh birthday. "The actual end was sudden," Dorothy wrote to her son, "but, as you know, he had been seriously ill and terribly depressed for the last eighteen months and his death was a merciful release, so you must not feel distressed either for him or me."[32]

The truth was, she could not help but feel that it had been a release for herself as well as for Mac. She did feel lonely without him—"I shall miss having him to look after, and there will be nobody to curse me and keep me up to the mark!"[33] she half joked to Muriel St. Clare Byrne—but at the same time, she no longer had to deal with his anger, his jealousy of her work, his nerves, or his demands. She invited her close friend Norah Lambourne, an artist and stage designer, to come and live with her for a while, and began the process of adjusting to a new life and new freedoms.

Jack Lewis, meanwhile, faced a situation that in some ways was very similar. He and Warren had continued to live with Mrs. Moore even as she became harder and harder to live with. Much like Mac Fleming, she grew increasingly ill, frail, and demanding, until Warren could hardly bear it, and even Jack, the more even-tempered and levelheaded brother, was hard-pressed to put up with her. Nonetheless, he kept her at The Kilns as long as he could, until ill health and senility finally mandated that she be placed in a nursing home. And after that, he went to visit her there nearly every day.

Janie King Moore passed away on January 12, 1951. Like Dorothy after Mac's death the year before, Jack felt something of a shamefaced sense of relief. He was well aware, as he admitted to Arthur Greeves, that his home had been a much more pleasant place ever since Mrs. Moore had gone to the nursing home.[34] And now that he was released from the burden of the daily visits, he felt a greater sense of freedom— though not complete freedom, for there was still one ongoing, significant worry. His brother's alcoholism was growing steadily worse.

Heavy drinking had been one of Warren's methods of coping with the tension in the house when Mrs. Moore was still there, but her absence did nothing to slow it down. He had long been, and continued to be, a support to Jack in many ways—among other things, he was an invaluable helper with the enormous amount of daily correspondence—but too much stress or responsibility would frequently lead to drinking binges, which would lead in turn to breakdowns, enforced rest, and intense guilt. Jack was compassionate and patient, but his brother's infirmity was a difficult burden to bear, and sometimes hampered his own hopes of getting away for a while.

Still, both Jack and Dorothy had a little more flexibility and liberty now, and also a little more time for getting together now and then. They had an enjoyable visit in early 1954 at Oxford. Dorothy met Warren during this visit (possibly for the first time), and the two got along famously—not least because they both had an interest in French history.

"[Warren] has been re-reading *Gaudy Night*—to prolong (in some sort) your visit," Jack wrote to Dorothy in March 1954.[35] Perhaps Jack had been rereading it himself, despite his initial dislike; later that year, he asked her (possibly in a teasing mood, knowing her mixed feelings about the poetry and worldview of Milton) if she realized that the opening of a sonnet her character Harriet wrote in that book* was very similar to a portion of one of Milton's sonnets.[36]

In large matters and small, then, they were being drawn closer together, becoming more reliant on each other's friendship and sympathy. And as both of them were dealing with the major changes in their lives, a new challenge arose for them both, one that they would have to meet head-on and together. Fortunately, it was just the sort of challenge they both thrived on.

"Two Unforgivable Sins"

In late 1953, writer Kathleen Nott published *The Emperor's Clothes*, a book-length polemic against some of the most prominent Christian writers of the day. The subtitle of her book left no doubt about her intentions: *An Attack on the Dogmatic Orthodoxy of T. S. Eliot, Graham Greene, Dorothy Sayers, C. S. Lewis, and Others.* (Just in case anyone was still in the dark, the book's cover featured caricatures of the four authors named in the subtitle.)

Nott wrote her book to "register her dismay," as the Zaleskis put it, at the religious influence wielded by the writers

*Coincidentally—*Gaudy Night* was written before Dorothy had met or even heard of Jack—the hill that Harriet sat on to write her sonnet overlooked The Kilns!

she named in the book's subtitle.[37] While Jack, Dorothy, and other Christians may have believed that Christianity was on the wane among intellectuals in the 1950s, Nott and many of her fellow atheists saw things very differently. They thought that Christian belief was on the rise—and that this was a dangerous and pernicious trend.

"To try . . . to make morality depend on the metaphysical dogma and the authority of the Church means the death of morality," Nott argued in her book. "Mr. Eliot and those who share his opinions do not want people to be moral except as the Church prescribes."[38]

Of C. S. Lewis and Dorothy L. Sayers specifically (Dorothy later quipped that Nott "consistently presented [them] together in a kind of double turn, like knockabout comedians in a fair-ground"[39]), Nott complained:

> In both may be discerned again and again a wish to discredit scientific thinking which springs from a profounder wish to make theology paramount again. They are both writers and broadcasters with considerable popular appeal; and if, as I hope to show, their apparent willingness to probe the most fundamental intellectual issues merely masks this underlying wish, their distractive performances serve to put objective and verifiable thought in greater popular danger than it already is.[40]

Or, as Dorothy would later observe wryly to Barbara Reynolds, "As somebody remarked . . . 'you,' meaning C. S. Lewis and me and some other malefactors, 'have committed the two unforgivable sins: you believe in God and your books sell.'"[41]

"I see we have been in the pillory together along with company which I enjoy less than yours," Jack wrote to Dorothy soon after Nott's book came out. "Have you read Miss Nott yet? And should I? I had hoped she might send us all (as someone said) UN complimentary copies, for I'm an Ulster Scot and don't like spending good siller [silver] on the lady."[42] Dorothy had not yet read the book either, "for the same reason. Why should one pay good money to hear oneself abused?"[43] As it happened, Jack had just been recommending his brother's new book about French history, *The Splendid Century*, to Dorothy, and she gleefully promised to buy it with the money that she might otherwise have spent on Nott's book.

But there was widespread interest in a debate between Nott and her ideological opponents. The Socratic Club at Oxford, in which Jack was active, offered to host one, but Dorothy, though she had great interest in the Socratic Club and even hoped to start one of her own, turned down the offer on behalf of herself and her fellow combatants. She was already involved in making arrangements with St. Anne's House in Soho, London, a group promoting the interaction of faith and culture, in which she was very active. A debate was set up there between Eliot, Jack, and Dorothy on one side and Nott on the other.

But at the last moment, Eliot pulled out, citing health concerns, and as a result Nott—who had only agreed to participate if he would be there, since she saw him as the main target of her book—withdrew as well. Since the event was already scheduled, Nott's friend G. S. Frazer agreed to stand in for her. (Dorothy's own efforts to find replacements for Nott came up short, as the philosophers and scientists she knew at Oxford were either Christians or sympathetic to Christianity—causing her to note whimsically that, indeed, "Christians seem to be getting very savage and plentiful of late."[44])

Frazer debated Jack and Dorothy in front of what their friend John Wren-Lewis, who was there, described as "a packed and lively audience." Wren-Lewis added, "Frazer opened his speech by saying that he felt like 'a tame lion thrown to ravening Christians,' but the general consensus afterwords [sic] was that he met his opponents with dovelike cooing rather than leonine roars."[45]

Jack had warned Dorothy beforehand that he was not much of a debater anymore, but this account suggests that he and she both held their own. No copies of Jack's remarks appear to be available now (he may have spoken from notes, as he sometimes did), but Dorothy's speech has been reprinted, and from it we can gather that she was indeed in a "roaring" state of mind. She ruthlessly dissected fault after fault in Nott's book, from her "totalitarian" claims to authority right down to her consistent failure to include Dorothy's middle initial when using her name. But she never lost sight of the bigger picture—Nott's criticisms of religion and the conflict that Nott posited between science and theology—and she tackled these things head-on with her usual mixture of bluntness, insight, humor, and humility. At the climax of her speech, she explained:

Miss Nott says:

No one can say that "the Church" as a whole has ever stood for truth and . . . charity.

Well, the church does in fact lay a good deal of stress, not only [on] truth, but on love and charity. . . . But it is no use talking as though love and charity were easy. You cannot buy them in the market and slap them on a situation like plasters. If Miss Nott were here now, she and I could establish the Kingdom of Heaven between ourselves immediately—that is, we could *if* we could. It is quite simple: she has only to love me as well as she loves herself, and I have only to love her as well as I love myself, and there is the Kingdom. It is as simple as that—but would it be easy? Acknowledging myself to be worm-eaten with original sin, I acknowledge that I might find it difficult; and although Miss Nott is presumably without sin (since she does not admit the existence of sinfulness), it is conceivable that for one reason or another she also might encounter a little difficulty. Yet it would be useless for her to protest that one cannot love an unlovable object, since charity is precisely a readiness to love the unlovable. That is the trouble with the Christian graces—that without Grace they are impossible.[46]

There seems to have been a general sense among their audience that Jack and Dorothy came out of the debate triumphantly. But in a larger sense, neither was feeling particularly triumphal. Neither was convinced, as Nott and her allies were, that Christianity was resurgent among the intellectual classes (or anywhere else, for that matter). Instead, both had the sense that they were standing for truths that, while still as true as they ever had been, were falling into obscurity—not just spiritual truths either, but truths of all kinds.

The Dinosaurs' Club

But that same year, there was a glimmer of light when Cambridge University offered Jack the chair of Medieval and Renaissance Literature—the sort of prestigious position for which Oxford had twice passed him over, precisely because of his open advocacy of such unfashionable truths. While Cambridge as a general rule was no more sympathetic to Jack's stances than Oxford was, many there were genuinely interested in including some diversity of thought.

At first, however, Jack turned down the position, not once but twice. He simply did not see any way to leave his brother on his own. Tolkien, who as an elector had helped arrange the offer for his old friend, persuaded him to change his mind, pointing out that he could still live at The Kilns with Warren and travel back and forth.[47]

So Jack gave his inaugural lecture at Cambridge on November 29, 1954, to a packed and appreciative audience. Dorothy, unable to go, had asked Barbara Reynolds—who at the time was the lecturer in Italian Literature and Language at Cambridge—to go and send her a report on how it went. The report was a good one, and Dorothy was pleased. "It sounds as though he had been on his best behaviour—he can sometimes be very naughty and provocative—but he probably thought that his Inaugural was not quite the right moment for such capers," she observed.[48]

What exactly she meant by "naughty and provocative" isn't clear. As we've seen, she could sometimes be a little harder on Jack than his behavior seemed to warrant, and she sometimes even seemed to project some of her own qualities onto him (having been more than a little provocative herself in their debate with Frazer!). What he did do in this lecture, as Colin Duriez puts it, was "set out a defense of 'Old Western values' that he and Tolkien had championed in their work."[49] He "defined the Old West by placing it in contrast to the modern world," and presented himself, with humility but without apology, as a "dinosaur" whose knowledge of that older world might be of some value to the current generation.

> If a live dinosaur dragged its slow length into the laboratory, would we not all look back as we fled? What a chance to know at last how it really moved and looked and smelled and what noises it made! And if the Neanderthaler could talk, then, though his lecturing technique might leave much to be desired, should we not almost certainly learn from him some things about him which the best modern anthropologist could never have told us? He would tell us without knowing he was telling. One thing I know: I would give a great deal to hear any ancient Athenian, even a stupid one, talking about Greek tragedy. He would know in his bones so much that we seek in vain. At any moment some chance phrase might, unknown to him, show us where modern scholarship had been on the wrong track for years.
>
> Ladies and gentlemen, I stand before you somewhat as that Athenian might stand. I read as a native texts that you must read as foreigners. . . . That way, where I fail as a critic, I may yet be useful as a specimen. I would even dare to go further. Speaking not only for myself but for all other Old Western men whom you may meet, I would say, use your specimens while you can. There are not going to be many more dinosaurs.[50]

When Dorothy finally had the chance to read this speech for herself, she was wholly delighted with it. The line about reading as a native what younger generations read as foreigners captured something that she had been feeling for some time herself. In fact, she and Muriel St. Clare Byrne had been discussing the feeling the very evening before she read Jack's lecture.

For it was not just relationships and circumstances that were shifting and changing around them. Dorothy was now sixty-one years old and Jack fifty-six (he had given the inaugural lecture on his birthday). They were coming to terms with the fact that the world they were still very much engaged in was far from the same world in which they had grown up and been educated. Ideas with which they were intimately familiar, underlying assumptions shared by their generation, were not just being called into question but were in many cases not even recognized. The land and the culture of which they were both natives had all but vanished.

In such a situation, it made sense that the few remaining natives might lean upon each other for comfort and affirmation. Differences of opinion about how much of the comedy in Dante to bring out, and what constituted comedy in Dante to begin with, must have suddenly looked much smaller when the rising generation seemed to be almost totally in the dark about how to tackle Dante in the first place. Thus, Dorothy was enormously pleased to find that Jack "had given us a perfect expression of our own experience," and signed herself "your obliged and appreciative fellow-dinosaur."[51] By the same token, Jack suggested to her that they "form a Dinosaurs' Club (with an annual dinner in the Victoria &

Albert)."[52] In a later letter, he affectionately addressed her as "sister Dinosaur."[53]

It shows something about how much they truly had in common that Dorothy genuinely grasped what Jack was saying and didn't mistake his feeling of being a "dinosaur" for a persecution complex. Others—even some of those who knew him best—sometimes made such a mistake about him. Tolkien, who lived and taught at Oxford like Jack, was well aware of what he called "the extraordinary animosity" there toward Jack, largely because of his apologetics work.[54] But those who did not live in that atmosphere were not always as aware of its pervasiveness and its effects. Owen Barfield knew of the criticism but felt that Jack overreacted to it—that he was, as the Zaleskis put it, "taking part in a sort of deliberate role-playing."[55] Long after Jack's death, Barfield would endorse the view of writer Alan Watts that Jack had shown "a certain ill-concealed glee in adopting an old-fashioned and unpopular position."[56]

One audience member at Jack's inaugural lecture who came away with a somewhat similar impression was Joy Davidman. The New York writer who had so enjoyed *Essays Presented to Charles Williams* was now living in England with her two young sons and seeing a good deal of Jack. A voracious reader of his books and a frequent correspondent, Joy had sought him out for advice, comfort, and friendship when her marriage to fellow writer Bill Gresham was in its death throes. Some observers suspected that she had sought him out hoping for more than that, but for the time being they were simply close friends.

Joy thought Jack's inaugural address "brilliant," but was rather amused by his talk of Neanderthals and dinosaurs.

How that man loves being in a minority, even a lost-cause minority! *Athanasius contra mundum*, or Don Quixote against the windmills. He talked blandly of "post-Christian Europe," which I thought rather previous of him. I sometimes wonder what he would do if Christianity really did triumph everywhere; I suppose he would have to invent a new heresy.[57]

Though Joy shared Jack's belief system, she was nearly seventeen years younger than he was, had not been a Christian as long as he had, and had lived most of her life in very different surroundings. She (and Barfield) may have had a good point when they observed that Jack seemed to enjoy the position of representative of a vanishing and much-maligned world. But as much as they both cared about him, they nevertheless could not wholly grasp just what the hostility at Oxford had been like for him, and how much of that "role" he seemed to be playing was self-defense and self-protection. He had, after all, been turned down twice for a promotion that he richly deserved, solely—by all accounts—because he was a popular Christian apologist, and that sort of thing was just not done by Oxford dons.

But Dorothy understood. She may not have been part of the day-to-day Oxford life anymore, but she knew very well what it was like to face hostility for being a Christian apologist. They had, not very long ago, literally faced it side by side. And her robust nature, like his, would rather charge joyously into battle than wallow in self-pity, anger, or sulkiness. They were genuinely fortunate to have each other to count on in such battles.

By this time, more than likely, Dorothy was beginning to understand something else as well. Like most of Jack's friends, she could hardly help noticing the increasing role that Joy Davidman was playing in his life. But as it would turn out, Dorothy had quite different feelings on the subject from many of Jack's other friends.

Six

"I Do Most Heartily Rejoice"

In Joy and Sorrow

I t is difficult to guess when Dorothy first began to suspect that
something beyond friendship was developing between Jack
and Joy. She had met Joy at the debate at St. Anne's, which
Joy had attended with her parents, who were visiting England
at the time. The two women hit it off. They were, in fact, very
much alike: outspoken, intelligent, gregarious, witty. Jack later
wrote that the two of them discussed detective fiction (possibly,
though not definitely, at this meeting). Joy, he reported, was
"relieved" to hear that Dorothy hadn't turned against the detective genre or tried to distance herself from her own mystery
stories but had simply decided she "had done all she could" in
that line and was ready to move on to other things.[1]

To her ex-husband, Bill Gresham, Joy reported:

Dorothy Sayers was at the debate too: she's enormously witty
and a very eloquent speaker, a forthright old lady who wears

147

rather mannish clothes and doesn't give a damn about her hairdo. Mother said if brains made a woman look like that she was glad she wasn't intellectual. How they do run to form, the dears, don't they.[2]

(As Joy had just been writing about what she considered to be her mother's outlandish fashion sense and general obsession with her own looks, this was more a jab at her mother than a remark on Dorothy's appearance!)

Around six months later, in April 1955, Jack recommended that Dorothy read Joy's book *Smoke on the Mountain: An Interpretation of the Ten Commandments*. On the surface, the recommendation was casual enough—just one of many that he had given her over the years—and, as she often did, she followed his advice and got the book. (At the book table at an Inklings conference held in Oxford and Cambridge, many years ago, I was shown Dorothy's copy of *Smoke on the Mountain*.)

But there were one or two things about the recommendation and about the book itself that might have made Dorothy raise an eyebrow, knowing Jack as she did. In his letter, he referred to Joy, in an elaborately nonchalant manner, as if the two women had never been introduced before. It appeared he had forgotten all about their meeting the previous year. For a man with his prodigious memory to have such a lapse must have seemed odd. And then, as Dorothy would have discovered when she bought the book, he had written a preface for it.

Dorothy had good reason to know how unusual this was. A couple of times she had asked Jack to write a preface, either for one of her own books or for someone else's, and he had always begged off, protesting that he usually never knew enough about the subject of the books to be able to write a preface worth reading. No amount of pushing or pleading could get him to change his mind. So his change in policy here would have gotten her attention, though she might not have been clear yet on what was behind it.

But she must certainly have guessed that something was up a few months after that, when one of Jack's letters to her ended with two postscripts:

P. S. Joy Gresham, who is in the unhappy position of having borrowed my house and then finding that a change in my plans commits her to having me as a guest, sends her regards. She did all this typing.
P .P. S. by J. G.—I wouldn't precisely call it an unhappy position, would you?[3]

Many of the people closest to Jack were pretty sure by now that something was up, and quite a few of them were unhappy about it. Tolkien and the other Inklings disliked Joy and were displeased by her increasing presence in Jack's life. It was particularly distressing for Tolkien, who as a Roman Catholic would have been absolutely opposed to a romance and potential marriage with a divorcée. But besides that, her forceful personality was not the kind of thing any of them much cared for in a woman. On this point Jack diverged from them; years of friendship with Dorothy L. Sayers and other strong, intellectual, opinionated women had developed in him a genuine enjoyment and appreciation of just such a female personality. (Only after Joy happened to meet the Tolkiens for the first time, in the hospital where Joy was being treated for cancer and Edith Tolkien for arthritis in 1960, was there "somewhat of a reconciliation" between Jack and Tolkien over the matter.[4])

This raises an intriguing question: Would there have been a marriage between Jack Lewis and Joy Davidman if there had not first been a friendship between Jack Lewis and Dorothy L. Sayers? Of course, we can't say for sure, but it does seem highly probable that their friendship helped prepare him for Joy. Dorothy's energy, exuberance, and bluntness were some of Jack's favorite things about her, and he perceived them as closely tied to her femininity, even though her way of dressing and presenting herself (at least from her thirties onward) was seen by many as more masculine than feminine. This was one of the many reasons his friendship with her was such a valuable experience for him. As Mary Stewart Van Leeuwen writes, "With regard to gender, it is likely that Lewis's slowly changing views owed much to the intellectual and Christian ties he forged with Dorothy L. Sayers."[5] When he met Joy, he did not have to try to form an appreciation of the personality that many of his male friends were not at all ready to appreciate. The ground had, so to speak, already been prepared over the past several years.

But there were still obstacles to overcome in his relationship with Joy. Jack himself had some religious scruples about remarriage after divorce, and this may have played a role in his slowness to recognize his feelings for her. Even when he agreed to marry her in the spring of 1956 to help her and her boys stay in England, he considered it a marriage in name only and kept it quiet.

All that began to change when Joy became seriously ill in October. Rushed to the hospital after a fall, she was diagnosed with cancer. It had begun in her breast and spread to her bones; Jack's friend Dr. Havard, who treated her, told them that she could not live long.[6] Only now did Jack truly begin to realize how much Joy meant to him. At this point, he decided he needed to publicize their marriage.

In a letter to Dorothy on December 24, he wrote:

You may see in the *Times* a notice of my marriage to Joy Gresham. She is in hospital (cancer) and not likely to live, but if she gets over this go she must be given a home here. You must not think that anything wrong is going to happen. Certain problems do not arise between a dying woman and an elderly man. What I am mainly acquiring is two (nice) stepsons. Pray for us all, and God bless you.[7]

Given the nature of their friendship—in which so much time, energy, and dialogue were devoted to spiritual and literary matters as opposed to personal ones—and given some of Jack's ideas about friendship ("of course we do not want to know our Friend's affairs at all," he insisted in *The Four Loves*[8]), it is entirely possible Jack did not know that Dorothy's own husband had once been divorced. Her feelings on the subject were naturally, therefore, a little different from what his had long been. She did believe in making every effort to preserve a marriage—and accordingly she had strenuously resisted divorce herself, even when her own marriage went sour—but she was not prepared to state that it was wrong in every case. Her own son—who now went by his middle name, Anthony—had gotten divorced after a brief marriage in his twenties, and Dorothy wrote to him after he told her the news:

If the thing is irreparable, I believe it is better to make a complete break and start again. Half-and-half separations are only a misery and a temptation, and I have never been able to accept that rigid view about divorce by which the Western Church is (unlike the Eastern) hag-ridden. If one tries one's best and fails, well, there it is—if one has *really* tried.[9]

So she would not have been likely to think anything "wrong" with Jack's marriage in any case. Whether Jack knew this or not, though, it is significant that Dorothy was one of the friends he chose to tell about the marriage. He did not tell Tolkien, though he probably wished that he could have.[10] At this difficult and sensitive moment, and after all the tension that his relationship with Joy had already caused among his circle, Jack gravitated to friends who liked his new wife and whom he instinctively felt would understand and sympathize.

Of course, the situation, as most of Jack's friends could have predicted, was not destined to remain as it was for long. Soon he was writing to Dorothy again to explain that "on examination," Joy's first marriage really wasn't valid at all in the eyes of the church, as her husband had been married before and *his* first wife was still living.[11] He had asked a friend, Father Peter Bide, to come and pray for her—and also to perform a second marriage service, this time a religious one rather than the civil ceremony they had had before. This would be, in his eyes, the real thing.

"When I last wrote to you I would not have wished this," he added. "You will gather (and may say 'guessed as much') that my feelings had changed. . . . I hope you give us your blessing; I know you'll give us your prayers."[12] At last, he appeared to be admitting he had been heading all along in a direction that those who knew him well had seen before he did.

Whatever Dorothy thought of his theological reasoning on the subject of divorce and remarriage, she apparently kept it to herself and simply expressed her congratulations and support, for Jack and Joy both "enjoyed . . . [very] much" her answering letter.[13] Unfortunately, that letter has been lost, so we can only guess at what she might have said. It's also interesting to guess at how she might have felt in general about the "rather frightened bachelor" getting married. Most likely, she would have been very glad. Marriage appeared to give Jack what she had long thought he needed: new insight and understanding of women, a lessening of the "complete blank" in that area she had sensed in him.

When he sent her a copy of his new novel, *Till We Have Faces*, which he had written with much input and help from Joy, Dorothy's remark to Barbara Reynolds was telling: "He has done the woman—one of those fierce, jealous, Florence-Nightingale types who wear everybody else to pieces—very well, I think" (though she could not resist adding, "bearing in mind . . . that it was rather bold of him to attempt it").[14] Dorothy did not live to see Jack's book *The Four Loves*, but if she had, she might have noted with approval that his view of headship in marriage had shifted quite a bit as well. No longer was he portraying it as an arrangement where the husband would cast the deciding vote—and, Dorothy doubtless would have noticed with glee, no longer was he taking a certain British epic poet's word for what it meant. Instead, he wrote:

Christian writers (notably Milton) have sometimes spoken of the husband's headship with a complacency to make the blood run cold. We must go back to our Bibles. The husband is the head of the wife just in so far as he is to her what

Christ is to the Church. He is to love her as Christ loved the Church—read on—*and give his life for her* (Eph. V, 25).[15]

What Jack did tell Dorothy about his experience of marriage were some of the most beautiful words he ever wrote. Very frequently, when the story of Jack Lewis and Joy Davidman's marriage has been told, these lines from one of Jack's letters to Dorothy have been quoted: "We have much gaiety and even some happiness. . . . My heart is breaking and I was never so happy before: at any rate there is more in life than I knew about."[16] A little later, he wrote to her, "If the medical were as good as the domestic situation I'd be the most fortunate man in England. . . . I have bad spasms of both body and soul [he was suffering from a bone disease, for which Dorothy recommended he try an osteopath], but they all go on amidst a sort of ballet of *agape, storge,* and *eros.*"[17]

These letters are, as Alan Jacobs notes, "uncharacteristically self-revealing."[18] He was opening up to Dorothy in ways that he never had before; his new and deep emotional experience was carrying over into other aspects of his life, including his friendship with her. He even told her what he had told very few people—the fact that Warren had been for some time an alcoholic.

Dorothy responded to his openness by opening up herself, in her own inimitable fashion. She and Jack were still following their old pattern in their letters of dealing with all other matters before they got to personal ones, so her letter of July 3, 1957, starts with her response to a point he had made about academic trends, then proceeds to respond to another point he'd made about Dante and astrology, and then goes into a lament that, because he has reported that his stepsons have pet mice, she won't be able to offer the Lewises one of the kittens her cats are constantly producing. "I have written you a poem instead," she announces, and offers a witty little sonnet, titled "The Cosmographers," about academic dinosaurs like herself and him, which she labels "wedding-present, slightly belated."

Only then, on the fourth page of her letter, does she add, with sudden soberness:

> I mustn't weary you with all this chat—Believe that I do most heartily rejoice with your joys + grieve with your griefs. With part of these I can especially sympathize, since whisky was my husband's trouble, which in the end destroyed him. It wasn't the kind of trouble one could do very much about— the chronic, steady sort, which made things rather trying sometimes. However, it's all over now, so I don't usually say anything about it. These things happen.[19]

The inclusion of this passage made it truly the most open, honest, and personal letter she had ever written to him. Sadly, it would also be one of the last.

Seven

"A Friend, Not an Ally"

Dorothy's translation of *The Song of Roland* came out that same year, 1957—she had actually taken a break from her beloved Dante to work on this poem, which took her back to her old studies in French. As she usually did with her new books, she sent Jack a copy. Thanking her for the gift, he remarked that certain details of the poem must have made it even more difficult to translate than Dante.

That was to be the last letter Jack would ever write to Dorothy. No answering letter exists, but we know she must have responded to what he wrote, either by letter or in person, for Jack would later reflect: "Her delight at this (surely not very profound) remark suggested that she was rather starved for rational criticism."[1]

The observation reminds us how fortunate each of them was to have the other to help provide such criticism. It was an integral and vital part of their friendship, something each

157

needed and valued. It was what helped to make theirs a true relationship of equals—a meeting of minds.

Less than three months after receiving that letter, on December 17, 1957, Dorothy L. Sayers died suddenly of a heart attack at her home in Witham, shortly after coming back from a day of Christmas shopping. She was sixty-four years old.

Jack Lewis's stepson Douglas Gresham recalls that the first time he ever saw Jack cry was when he heard about Dorothy's death. Douglas's mother, Joy, cried as well.[2] For her, though she had known Dorothy only a couple of years and rarely saw her in person, it was the loss of someone she liked and admired. For Jack, it was a much greater loss: the loss of a trusted and beloved friend, colleague, and confidante all in one.

Over the years they had helped, educated, guided, teased, critiqued, chastised, defended, consoled, and laughed with each other. He had treasured their correspondence, delighted in their meetings, and after many years had learned to share with her his deepest feelings. In some ways, though he may not have realized it, she had taught him aspects of friendship that even this man who was so rich in friends had not fully understood; by the end, for instance, she had shown him that friends *did* care something about each other's personal affairs, after all.

Theirs was, ultimately, the kind of friendship in Christ that Aimee Byrd writes about in *Why Can't We Be Friends?*, which involves both encouragement and exhortation, "two sides of the same coin. Both of them share the goal of promoting holiness. Encouragement gives support and stimulates courage so the recipient can act on true hope. . . . Exhortation can be toward a positive action or against a negative action or sin."[3] All this they had done for each other.

Life without their vibrant interactions would never again be quite the same. No more of her letters would "shine" on his desk and give a lift to his spirits; he would never again have the chance to face head-on the "high wind" of her personality that was for him such a tonic.

A Surprise and a Tribute

Close upon the grief came a surprise. Dorothy's son, Anthony, was in his thirties by this time. Theirs had never been a conventional relationship, but she had helped him through the years in every way she could—sending financial support, even well into adulthood, whenever he needed it; offering him advice; encouraging his academic and professional efforts; even sending constructive criticism of the occasional poems and plays at which he tried his hand—and made him sole beneficiary in her will. She had done, Anthony believed, "the very best she could."[4]

Still, she had continued to keep her son's existence a secret from nearly everyone she knew, even her closest friends. Now that she was gone and funeral arrangements had to be made, he began to make himself known to those friends.

In Barbara Reynolds's biography of Sayers, we have one example of how he did this from Muriel St. Clare Byrne—who had already unknowingly met him once in his childhood, when she and Dorothy had gone on vacation together.

Muriel recalled arriving one evening at a cottage in an Oxfordshire village. Dorothy disappeared inside for a short while, then came out again and invited Muriel in. She remembered meeting Ivy and seeing a girl (Isobel) [another of Ivy's foster children] and a boy of about ten years of age. This was John [Anthony]. Muriel had no idea that he was Dorothy's son and she did not see him again until the day after Dorothy's death, when their meeting was indeed dramatic. He arrived on the doorstep of her house in London, a young man of thirty-three, and asked, "Are you Miss St Clare Byrne?" "Yes," Muriel answered. The unknown young man then said, "I am Dorothy Sayers' son. May I come in?"[5]

Thinking back to their first meeting, Muriel recalled that as they left Ivy's cottage she had noticed Dorothy was in tears.

Another friend Anthony soon got in touch with was Jack Lewis. Jack was asked—whether by Anthony himself or someone else is not clear—to speak at Dorothy's funeral, but he was not able to attend. But he wrote and sent a "panegyric" (similar in form and tone to a eulogy), which was read at the service by George Bell, the Lord Bishop of Chichester.[6]

According to Walter Hooper, Anthony wrote afterward to thank Jack for the panegyric.[7] From Jack's reply, it appears it was his recurring and painful bone disease that had kept him home from Dorothy's funeral. In the thank-you letter (now apparently lost), Anthony seems to have expressed his condolences on Jack's "affliction," for Jack answered, "'Affliction' is too strong a word for my bone trouble. 'Nuisance' is about all I can claim for it. Your loss is a real affliction, on which I offer my sympathy."[8]

The panegyric itself is extremely characteristic of Jack and of his friendship with Dorothy. Unlike most such funeral orations, which concentrate on the emotional and the personal, this one focused mainly on her work and her intellect, her primary points of contact with Jack—and indeed with the world. (The very first sentence reads: "The variety of Dorothy Sayers's work makes it almost impossible to find anyone who can deal properly with it all."[9]) In fact, it was in many ways more like one of their old friendly wrangles than a eulogy for the departed.

In this speech, Jack showed just how well he had come to understand Dorothy—in some ways, perhaps, better than she understood herself—in much the same way as she had understood him. That understanding was so comprehensive it applied even to areas of her life and work he was not well acquainted with. For instance, though he admitted freely to having little liking for detective stories, he showed here a better grasp of hers than many of the greatest Wimsey fans.

> I have heard it said that Lord Peter is the only imaginary detective who ever grew up. . . . Reviewers complained that Miss Sayers was falling in love with her hero. On which a better critic remarked to me, "It would be true to say she was falling out of love with him; and ceased fondling a girl's dream—if she had ever done so—and began inventing a man."[10]

From there he went on to recall her attitude toward her writing in general.

> She always saw herself as one who has learned a trade, and respects it, and demands respect for it from others. We who loved her may (among ourselves) lovingly admit that this attitude was sometimes almost comically emphatic. . . . She aspired to be, and was, at once a popular entertainer and a

conscientious craftsman: like (in her degree) Chaucer, Cer-
vantes, Shakespeare, or Molière. I have an idea that, with a
very few exceptions, it is only such writers who matter much
in the long run.[11]

This passage is highly reminiscent of the pattern found in
many of Jack's letters to Dorothy about her work: thoughtful
criticism mingled with enthusiastic appreciation. One can
easily imagine her ready to fight him over "almost comically
emphatic," but at the same time, she no doubt would have
properly appreciated the comparison to some of the greatest
writers who had ever lived.

His next point showed a truly remarkable insight into her
character.

For a Christian, of course, this pride in one's craft, which so
easily withers into pride in oneself, raises a fiercely practical problem. It is delightfully characteristic of her extremely
robust and forthright nature that she soon . . . made it the
theme of one of her major works. The architect in *The Zeal
of Thy House* is at the outset the incarnation of . . . a possible
Dorothy whom the actual Dorothy Sayers was offering for
mortification.[12]

This architect, William of Sens, Jack explained, is a master
craftsman who justly feels pride in his work and makes it his
most important priority. "But she knows," Jack added, "that,
without grace, it is a dangerous virtue: little better than the
'artistic conscience' which every Bohemian bungler pleads as
a justification for neglecting his parents, deserting his wife,
and cheating his creditors."[13]

Dorothy might have been ready to fight him all over again at his disparaging usage of "artistic conscience," the very concept that she had insisted he take more seriously during their spat back in 1946. Yet the larger point he was making shows his very real understanding of and appreciation for his friend's humility, honesty, and self-awareness. And it was these qualities in her, he was suggesting, that raised her ideas about "artistic conscience" above the normal worldly definition of the term. She believed that the artist must serve the work faithfully, but that ultimately, in doing so, he or she was serving Someone higher than the work.

This point actually contains echoes of a letter she had written to him not long after that 1946 argument, in which she reflected on how both William in Zeal and Judas in The Man Born to Be King exemplified the sin of pride, and how frustrated she was that some of her most devout Christian audience members didn't seem to realize that pride was such a terrible sin—they thought surely it was not as terrible as, for instance, adultery or greed![14] Her complaint about this shows just how well she understood the sin of pride and how dangerous she recognized it to be. The character of Judas, too, who is so proud that he thinks he knows better than Jesus Himself how salvation must be accomplished, is in some ways "a possible Dorothy." But it took Jack Lewis, a fellow writer and a good friend, to recognize and to point out just what a "robust and forthright nature" it took to do what she did with these characters: to make herself not the hero of her own works, as so many lesser writers do, but at best the antihero—and at worst the villain.

From there, Jack went on to emphasize, seriously and respectfully, the distinctions that had mattered so much to Dorothy.

She never sank the artist and entertainer in the evange-
list. . . . Of course, while art and evangelism were distinct,
they turned out to demand one another. Bad art on this theme
went hand in hand with bad theology.[15]

He quoted her extensively on the subject, and then he
pointed to the great paradox of her career: "Her disclaimer
of an intention to 'do good' was ironically rewarded by the
immense amount of good she evidently did."[16]

In the final section of the panegyric, Jack paid tribute to
the translating work that had so absorbed Dorothy in the
last few years of her life, primarily the Dante translation. He
acknowledged the differences of opinion between them over
her tone and style, but added that "she had risen" so much in
the second part of the translation, the *Purgatorio*, that he had
had "great hopes of her *Paradiso*." He concluded:

Well. She died instead; went, as one may in all humility hope,
to learn more of Heaven than even the *Paradiso* could tell her.
For all she did and was, for delight and instruction, for her
militant loyalty as a friend, for courage and honesty, for the
richly feminine qualities which showed through a port and
manner superficially masculine and even gleefully ogreish—
let us thank the Author who invented her.[17]

That conclusion mingled together so many of the different
elements of their fifteen-year friendship: the professional and
the personal, the masculine and the feminine, the spiritual
and the literary. It was, again, unconventional. There was
nothing of flattery in it, no feel-good sentiments; surely it
was one of very few eulogies in the history of the genre to

use the adjective *ogreish*. But the word was no accident and certainly no insult. The entire speech was, typically for Jack, precise in its word choice and utterly sincere in its respect, gratitude, and admiration. And as Anthony Fleming seems to have assured him, it was very much appreciated by those at the service.[18] Doubtless the qualities to which Jack lovingly paid tribute were qualities recognized and loved by Dorothy's family and her other friends as well.

The Question of Influence

Joy and Jack Lewis both outlived Dorothy L. Sayers by only a few years. Joy succumbed to cancer on July 13, 1960, at the age of forty-five. Jack was nearly sixty-five when he died, on November 22, 1963, of kidney failure. But he lived long enough to see other writers beginning to reflect on the legacy of himself and his circle of friends and to set the record straight when those writers got some of the details wrong. Primarily, those details included who exactly was involved in the Inklings and how they influenced one another.

In January 1963, Jack wrote a letter to the editor of *Encounter* to correct a few such details in John Wain's book *Sprightly Running*. Wain had been a pupil of Jack's at Oxford and had met the Inklings, though he was not a member. In his book, he had mentioned several "alliances" formed by the Inklings, including Dorothy L. Sayers. But Jack pointed out that the only two Inklings Dorothy had ever known were himself and Charles Williams. He also pointed out, gently but firmly, that she was "a friend, not an ally."[19]

Then there was the question of influence. Jack's observation on Tolkien's lack of susceptibility to it—"you might as well try to influence a bandersnatch"—is well known.[20] In fact, Jack expressed serious doubts about whether there was much influence going on among his friends in general. In the same letter in which he dismissed his influence on Tolkien, he wrote of Dorothy, "I am sure she neither exerted nor underwent any literary influence at all. Of course it may be that . . . I don't see (objectively) what was really going on."[21]

It's quite possible that he didn't. Of course, if he was referring only to the "literary" type of influence, it's true that neither Jack nor Dorothy influenced each other's literary style very much. Each had a distinct and well-developed voice by the time they met, which no amount of reading or discussion with fellow writers could do much to alter. Yet there's more to influence than that. Perhaps Tolkien was on the right track when, asked about this matter of influence among his writing friends, he responded, "The unpayable debt that I owe to [Lewis] was not influence as it is ordinarily understood, but sheer encouragement." As Diana Pavlac Glyer points out, "Here Tolkien is very careful in his wording: he does not say that encouragement is not influence." In fact, she argues, "it is time that encouragement and support be accepted as transforming aspects of influence."[22]

Jack and Dorothy might very well have accepted that definition of influence in the context of their long professional and personal relationship. Each of them had spent a significant amount of time listening to each other, bouncing ideas off each other, absorbing each other's thoughts. Even in situations where each stubbornly insisted on sticking with his or her own point of view, they could not help but be affected by each other's arguments and ideas.

As we have seen, on points where they did agree, Dorothy helped Jack to find more confidence in his own viewpoint. In turn, as they grew to know each other better, he was frequently able to offer her understanding and encouragement in her role as translator as well as that of apologist, being one of the rare figures who could grasp and appreciate the challenges of both. (In response to her translation of the *Purgatorio*, he dubbed her "*grante translateuse*"—medieval French for "great translator"—a compliment that she must have appreciated very much.[23]) Each proved to be a loyal supporter and defender of the other—sometimes at moments when such support was very much needed. And, bottom line, they had liked each other, and liked and appreciated each other's work. That alone meant a great deal to two "dinosaurs" who had grown used to misunderstanding and criticism, sometimes even from those closest to them.

In May 1963, about six months before his death, Jack Lewis was interviewed by Sherwood Wirt of *Decision*, the magazine of the Billy Graham Evangelistic Association. Among other things, Wirt asked Lewis which Christian books had helped him. Jack answered, "The contemporary book that has helped me the most is Chesterton's *The Everlasting Man*. Others are Edwyn Bevan's book, *Symbolism and Belief*, Rudolf Otto's *The Idea of the Holy*, and the plays of Dorothy Sayers."[24]

He meant, no doubt, *The Man Born to Be King*, the play cycle that had moved him to tears, that had become part of his regular Lenten reading, and that he had written to Dorothy to tell her, every now and then throughout the years of their friendship, he had just been reading again. For a man as widely read and as devout as C. S. Lewis to love these plays so much that he made them a recurring part of his devotional reading, and listed them among the few books that had helped him the most in his spiritual life, was a magnificent tribute.

And this brings us back to the question of influence. It is not hard to imagine that a play cycle about the life, death, and resurrection of Jesus that Jack read so often, and that he said helped him so much, played a key role in the development of his own ideas about Jesus. Dorothy had a gift for making a completely good character—including this best of all characters—utterly charismatic and compelling. It was a gift that would have been fully appreciated by Jack Lewis, who had written in "A Preface to *Paradise Lost*" about how much easier it was, in a world where we are all fallen, to make a bad character relatable and compelling (using Milton's Satan as an example).

But Dorothy presented the Savior of the world as someone set apart by His sinless divinity, worthy of awe and reverence, "sharp and stern and bracing,"[25] and yet still truly human and lovable. As she has Mary Magdalene say to the apostle John, "The Master's the only good man I ever met who knew how miserable it felt to be bad. It was as if he got right inside you, and *felt* all the horrible things you were doing to yourself."[26]

Dorothy's plays are not read (let alone performed) nearly as much nowadays as they once were; those of us who love them would say that they're not read nearly often enough. Yet one could justifiably argue that they are still influencing the world through the works of one of their biggest fans. The Jesus who moved C. S. Lewis to tears in those plays undoubtedly shines through in his bestselling apologetic works, and probably also in Aslan, his great fictional representation of

Christ. Like Dorothy's Jesus, Aslan is both stern and gentle, intimidating and playful, and wholly lovable. Jack could conceivably have come up with that characterization all on his own—he was both spiritual enough and talented enough for that—but *The Man Born to Be King* had left such a great impression on his mind and heart that it must have played some sort of role in shaping his most beloved character and his faith in general.

And it's worth noting that this same portrayal of Jesus that Dorothy created, which meant so much to Jack, exemplified what Dorothy saw as ideal interactions between men—specifically, one Man—and women. She had famously written of Jesus in her essay "The Human-Not-Quite-Human":

> Perhaps it is no wonder that women were first at the Cradle and last at the Cross. They had never known a man like this Man—there never has been such another. A prophet and teacher who never nagged at them, never flattered or coaxed or patronised; who never made arch jokes about them, never treated them either as "The women, God help us!" or "The ladies, God bless them!"; who rebuked without querulousness and praised without condescension; who took their questions and arguments seriously; who never mapped out their sphere for them, never urged them to be feminine or jeered at them for being female; who had no axe to grind and no uneasy male dignity to defend; who took them as he found them and was completely unself-conscious.[27]

This was the way Dorothy saw Jesus treating women in the Gospels and the way she wished His church would treat women. Her portrayal of Him, emphasizing these qualities, could not help but develop and enrich Jack's view of women as well as his view of Jesus Himself.

A Last Word from Dorothy

Jack was fortunate to have a chance to pay a final tribute to the woman whose work and friendship had been such a great blessing to him. Obviously, in any friendship that lasts until one party's death, the friend who lives longer gets to have the last word. But it seems a shame that we can never know exactly what a panegyric by Dorothy L. Sayers for C. S. Lewis might have included. To imagine her in dialogue with his panegyric for her, as I have done here, is an interesting and helpful exercise, but in the end it's still only speculation.

What we can do is look back through her writings to him and about him to be reminded of the things she liked and appreciated most about him: his imagination, his humor, his value as both appreciative listener and sparring partner, the understanding and sympathy he could offer her as a fellow "dinosaur," and the strong and robust faith that, in the final analysis, was so like her own.

Perhaps it's a 1947 letter to their mutual friend Brother George Every that best sums up Dorothy's thoughts on Jack. Like the eulogy Jack would one day write for her—like most of their thoughts about each other—it mingles thoughtful criticism with sincere praise. But her final, admiring word on him in this letter is so irresistible that I will let it be her final word on him in this book.

But Lewis is magnificently ruthless with the people who do set out to produce what purports to be a logical argument and then fake the premises, or beg the question, or leave their middles undistributed, or use ambivalent terms, or smuggle the concept of time into an argument about eternity, or ignorantly confuse efficient causes with final causes and attribute the resulting absurdity to St. Thomas. He is down on the thing like a rat; he is God's terrier, and I wouldn't be without him for the world.[28]

Timeline

Note: There may have been more meetings between C. S. Lewis and Dorothy L. Sayers than we're aware of. The ones listed here are those mentioned in their correspondence or by other sources.

1893 • June 13: Dorothy Leigh Sayers is born to Rev. Henry and Helen Sayers in Oxford, England.

1898 • January: Dorothy moves with her family to Bluntisham.

1898 • November 29: Clive Staples "Jack" Lewis is born to Albert and Flora Lewis in Belfast, Ireland.

1905 Jack moves with his family to the outskirts of Belfast, to a house called Little Lea.

1908 August 23: Flora Lewis dies of cancer.

September: Jack is sent to Wynyard School in Watford, Hertfordshire, England, with his older brother, Warren.

1909 January 17: Dorothy is sent to the Godolphin School in Salisbury, England.

1910 March 23: Dorothy is confirmed with her Godolphin School class at Salisbury Cathedral.

September: Jack is sent to Campbell College, Belfast, Ireland.

1911 Jack is sent to school at Cherbourg House, Malvern, England.

1912 Jack loses his childhood faith.

October 11: Having won a scholarship, Dorothy begins her studies at Somerville College, Oxford.

1913   September: Jack is sent to school at Malvern College, Malvern, England.

1914   September 19: Jack begins his studies with W. T. Kirkpatrick at Great Bookham.

December 6: Jack is confirmed at St. Mark's Church near Belfast.

1915   June: Dorothy finishes her college course with first-class honors in French.

1916   January 18: Dorothy begins a teaching job in Hull.

December 28: Dorothy publishes her first book, *Op. 1.*

1917   April 26: Having won a scholarship, Jack arrives at University College, Oxford, to begin his studies and his military training.

April 27: Dorothy arrives back in Oxford, to begin work at Blackwell Publishing on May 1.

April 30: Jack joins the Officers' Training Corps.

November 29: Jack arrives at the French front.

1918   April 15: Jack is wounded at the Battle of Arras.

1919   March: Jack publishes his first book, *Spirits in Bondage*.

September: Dorothy takes a position as assistant to Eric Whelpton at L'Ecole des Roches in Normandy, France, which lasts about a year; she spends the next few years after that in various teaching jobs in England.

December: Jack is officially discharged from the army.

1920   October 14: Dorothy is awarded BA and MA degrees from Oxford (among the first women to receive degrees there).

1921   June: Jack takes up residence with Mrs. Janie King Moore, mother of his late army friend Paddy Moore, and her daughter, Maureen.

1922   May: Dorothy begins work at S. H. Benson's advertising agency in London, where she remains for nine years.

1923 Dorothy publishes *Whose Body?*, her first novel and the beginning of her highly successful Lord Peter Wimsey series.

March (or thereabouts): Dorothy becomes pregnant by Bill White.

1924 January 3: Dorothy gives birth to her son, John Anthony White (eventually known as Anthony Fleming).

January 31: John Anthony is sent to live with Dorothy's aunt and cousin, Amy and Ivy Shrimpton.

1925 May 20: Jack is elected a Fellow of Magdalen College, Oxford.

1926 April 13: Dorothy marries Oswald Atherton "Mac" Fleming.

1929 Trinity Term (the Oxford term following Easter): Jack embraces theism.

September 25: Albert Lewis, not long after being diagnosed with colon cancer, dies of cardiac arrest in Belfast.

1930 • October: Jack, his brother Warren, and Mrs. Moore jointly purchase The Kilns, a house in Oxford, which they move into on October 10.

1931 • September 28: About a week after a long talk on the subject with J. R. R. Tolkien and Hugo Dyson, Jack converts to Christianity.

1932 • December 21: Warren Lewis retires from the army.

1933 • The Inklings begin to meet regularly at The Eagle and Child pub in Oxford and at Jack's rooms in Magdalen College.

1941 • June 25: First mention of Jack in one of Dorothy's letters (repeated references to *The Problem of Pain*).

• Dorothy publishes *The Mind of the Maker*, in which she quotes Jack.

• December 23: First mention of Dorothy in one of Jack's letters (thoughts on *The Mind of the Maker* and *Gaudy Night*).

1942   Early April: Dorothy writes her first letter to Jack.

Sometime in April: Jack first writes to Dorothy.

June 2 or 3: Probably the date of Dorothy and Jack's first meeting, in Oxford.

1944   November or December: Dorothy begins translating Dante's *Divine Comedy*, a project that will occupy her for the rest of her life.

1945   May 15: Charles Williams, a friend of both Jack and Dorothy, dies at the Acland Hospital in Oxford.

May 17: Jack asks Dorothy to contribute to the memorial volume *Essays Presented to Charles Williams*, to be edited by himself.

1947   December 4: *Essays Presented to Charles Williams* is published by Oxford University Press.

1949   Mid-August: Jack hosts a party for Dorothy while she is at Oxford to lecture on Dante for the Summer School of Italian Studies.

October: Last regular meeting of the Inklings.

November 16: Dorothy's translation of Dante's *Inferno*, the first volume of *The Divine Comedy*, is published by Penguin Classics.

1950 January: Joy Davidman Gresham writes her first letter to Jack.

June 9: Mac Fleming dies at home in Witham of a cerebral hemorrhage.

1951 January 12: Janie King Moore dies at the Restholme Nursing Home in Oxford of influenza.

1952 August: On a visit to England, Joy meets Jack and Warren.

1954 February 18 (or thereabouts): Dorothy visits Jack at Oxford and meets Warren (possibly for the first time).

October 24: Jack and Dorothy debate G. S. Frazer at St. Anne's House, Soho, London, over Kathleen Nott's book *The Emperor's Clothes*; Dorothy and Joy Davidman meet at the debate.

November 29: Having accepted the Chair of Medieval and Renaissance Literature at Cambridge University, Jack delivers his inaugural lecture there on his fifty-sixth birthday.

1955 Dorothy's translation of the *Purgatorio*, the second volume of the *Divine Comedy*, is published by Penguin Classics.

May 10: Jack and Dorothy cosign a letter to the *Times* of London to call attention to the tenth anniversary of Charles Williams's death.

1956 April 23: Jack and Joy undergo a civil marriage to allow Joy and her children to stay in England.

May 9 (or thereabouts): Jack and Dorothy meet for lunch at Cambridge.

October 18: Joy breaks her leg and is taken to the hospital, where she is diagnosed with cancer.

December 24: Jack informs Dorothy of his marriage to Joy.

1957 March 21: Jack and Joy undergo a second (religious) marriage service in the hospital.

June 25: Jack tells Dorothy of the second marriage service.

December 17: Dorothy dies at home in Witham of a coronary thrombosis.

1958 January 15: Jack's tribute, "A Panegyric for Dorothy L. Sayers," is read by George Bell, Lord Bishop of Chichester, at Dorothy's memorial service at St. Margaret's Church, London.

1960 July 13: Joy dies at the Radcliffe Hospital in Oxford of cancer.

1963 November 22: Jack dies at The Kilns of kidney failure.

Acknowledgments

First of all, thanks go to the wonderful team at the Marion E. Wade Center at Wheaton College, who did all they could to help with this project, including giving me a 2018 Clyde S. Kilby Research Grant. Thanks to Crystal and David Downing and to Marjorie Lamp Mead for their unflagging support and valuable insight. Thanks to Elaine Hooker and the Reading Room staff who helped with my research in the Center's archives.

Thanks to Rachel Churchill at the C. S. Lewis Company Ltd., to Georgia Glover at David Higham Associates, to Jake Allgeier at Open Road Media, and to HarperCollins Publishers for permission to publish excerpts from the works and letters of Lewis and Sayers.

At Baker Books, thanks to Bob Hosack, Lindsey Spoolstra, Patti Brinks, Olivia Peitsch, Janelle Wiesen, Melanie Burkhardt, Erin Bartels, and Eileen Hanson for all their hard work. At Foundry Literary + Media, thanks to my agent, Chris Park.

One of the best aspects of researching and writing about Dorothy L. Sayers and C. S. Lewis is being part of the communities of their devoted fans. Some of these groups are separate, some overlap, but all have been warm and supportive. I've loved meeting you in person, chatting with you online, and working with you on podcasts and other projects in honor of the writers who mean so much to us. Special thanks to Douglas Gresham, William O'Flaherty, Crystal Hurd, Alan Snyder, and Corey Latta. There are too many more to name here, but please know how grateful I am for each one of you and for your encouragement. Special thanks go to Laura K. Simmons and Gary L. Tandy for their article "Books, Theology, and Hens: The Correspondence and Friendship of C. S. Lewis and Dorothy L. Sayers" (in *Faculty Publications*, [June 5, 2016], George Fox University Department of English), which was invaluable.

Finally, thanks as always to my family, friends, and godchildren for your love and support. Special thanks to Mom and Dad, who made sure I remembered to do things like eat and sleep, and thus ensured that I survived to complete this book. I literally (and you know I'm not one to use *literally* lightly!) could not have done it without you.

Notes

Introduction

1. Lewis to Dorothy L. Sayers, December 14, 1945, *The Collected Letters of C. S. Lewis*, vol. 2, ed. Walter Hooper, *Books, Broadcasts, and the War 1931–1949* (New York: HarperCollins, 2004), 682.

2. Sayers to C. S. Lewis, May 13, 1943, *The Letters of Dorothy L. Sayers*, vol. 2, ed. Barbara Reynolds, *1937 to 1943: From Novelist to Playwright* (New York: St. Martin's Press, 1997), 413.

3. Barbara Reynolds, "C. S. Lewis and Dorothy L. Sayers," remarks made at the C. S. Lewis Summer Institute, Cambridge, 1998, repr. in *C. S. Lewis Remembered*, ed. Harry Lee Poe and Rebecca Whitten Poe (Grand Rapids: Zondervan, 2006), 195–96.

4. Justin Phillips, *C. S. Lewis at the BBC: Messages of Hope in the Darkness of War* (London: HarperCollins, 2002), 199–200.

5. C. S. Lewis, *The Four Loves*, in *The Inspirational Writings of C. S. Lewis* (New York: Inspirational Press, 1994), 246.

6. Aimee Byrd, *Why Can't We Be Friends?: Avoidance Is Not Purity* (Phillipsburg, NJ: P & R Publishing, 2018), 35.

Chapter 1 "No Mean City"

1. See Luke Barratt, "Oxford in World War I," *Cherwell*, July 28, 2014, http://cherwell.org/2014/07/28/oxford-in-world-war-i/.

2. Lewis to Albert Lewis, April 28, 1917, *The Collected Letters of C. S. Lewis*, vol. 1, ed. Walter Hooper, *Family Letters 1905–1931* (San Francisco: HarperSanFrancisco, 2004), 295.

3. Sayers to Henry and Helen Sayers, April 28, 1917, *The Letters of Dorothy L. Sayers*, vol. 1, ed. Barbara Reynolds, *1899 to 1936: The Making of a Detective Novelist* (New York: St. Martin's Press, 1996), 129.

4. Dorothy L. Sayers, "My Edwardian Childhood," in *Dorothy L. Sayers: Child and Woman of Her Time, A Supplement to the Letters of Dorothy L. Sayers*, ed. Barbara Reynolds (Cambridge: The Dorothy L. Sayers Society, 2002), 3.

5. Dorothy L. Sayers, *Gaudy Night* (New York: HarperPerennial, 1993), 30.

6. Sayers, *Gaudy Night*, 287. "Restoring a lost breathing," in a nutshell, refers to rediscovering how a word in a given language used to be pronounced.

7. C. S. Lewis, *Surprised by Joy*, in *The Inspirational Writings of C. S. Lewis* (New York: Inspirational Press, 1994), 101.

8. George Sayer, *Jack: A Life of C. S. Lewis* (Wheaton, IL: Crossway, 1994), 120.

9. Lewis, *Surprised by Joy*, 108.

10. C. S. Lewis, *The Lion, the Witch and the Wardrobe* (New York: HarperTrophy, 1978), 131.

11. Joseph Loconte, *A Hobbit, a Wardrobe, and a Great War* (Nashville: Nelson, 2015), 169.

12. Wilfred Owen, "Anthem for Doomed Youth," *The Poems of Wilfred Owen*, ed. Jon Stallworthy (New York: W. W. Norton, 1986), https://www.poetryfoundation.org/poems/47393/anthem-for-doomed-youth.

13. Loconte, *A Hobbit, a Wardrobe, and a Great War*, 101.

14. Loconte, *A Hobbit, a Wardrobe, and a Great War*, 101.

15. Barbara Reynolds, editor's note, in *Letters of Dorothy L. Sayers*, 1:91.

16. See page 20 of Barbara Reynolds, *Dorothy L. Sayers: Her Life and Soul* (1993) for a photo of teenage Dorothy in full costume as Athos, complete with wig, mustache, and plumed hat. The original photo is in the Marion E. Wade Center.

17. Sayers to Henry and Helen Sayers, August 3, 1914, *Letters of Dorothy L. Sayers*, 1:93.

18. Dorothy L. Sayers, *Whose Body?* (New York: HarperPaperbacks, 1995), 142.

19. Lewis, *Surprised by Joy*, 37.

20. Alan Jacobs, *The Narnian: The Life and Imagination of C. S. Lewis* (New York: HarperOne, 2005), 356.

21. Lewis, *Surprised by Joy*, 89.

22. The complete letter is not included in the first volume of *The Letters of Dorothy L. Sayers*, though it is mentioned (p. 35). This quote is taken from Barbara Reynolds, *Dorothy L. Sayers: Her Life and Soul* (New York: St. Martin's Griffin, 1993), 39. There, Reynolds says the letter was undated, but when she mentions it in the *Letters*, she gives it a date of February 13, 1910.

23. Reynolds, *Dorothy L. Sayers: Her Life and Soul*, 39.

24. Sayers to Henry and Helen Sayers, March 23, 1910, *Letters of Dorothy L. Sayers*, 1:40–41.

25. Sayers to Ivy Shrimpton, April 15, 1930, *Letters of Dorothy L. Sayers*, 1:306.

26. Sayers, "Cat o'Mary," in *Dorothy L. Sayers: Child and Woman of Her Time*, 117.

27. As evidence of this, Dorothy once recorded that someone had actually written to ask her, "Could you please tell me the title of the book in which Lord Peter rescues you from being condemned for murder." See Sayers to Barbara Reynolds, April 15, 1955, *Letters of Dorothy L. Sayers*, vol. 4, ed. Barbara Reynolds, *1951 to 1957: In the Midst of Life* (Cambridge: The Dorothy L. Sayers Society, 2000), 225.

28. Reynolds, *Letters of Dorothy L. Sayers*, 4:113.

29. Sayers to Henry and Helen Sayers, undated but marked third week in February 1909, *Letters of Dorothy L. Sayers*, 1:18.

30. G. K. Chesterton, *Orthodoxy: The Romance of Faith* (New York: Image Books, 1990), 101.

31. Sayers to Mrs. G. K. (Frances) Chesterton, June 15, 1936, *Letters of Dorothy L. Sayers*, 1:394.

32. Lewis, *Surprised by Joy*, 100.

33. Joseph Pearce, "Chesterton, Tolkien and Lewis in Elfland," *The Imaginative Conservative*, July 15, 2015, http://www.theimaginativeconservative.org/2015/07/chesterton-tolkien-and-lewis-in-elfland.html.

34. See Sayer, *Jack*, 143, and Reynolds, *Dorothy L. Sayers: Her Life and Soul*, 81, for publication dates and other details.

35. Sayers, "Desdichado," *Catholic Tales and Christian Songs* (Oxford: B. H. Blackwell, 1919), http://digital.library.upenn.edu/women/sayers/cathtales/dls-cathtales.html. Ellipses in original.

36. See Bryana Johnson, "Desdichado," *Having Decided to Stay*, October 22, 2012, https://bryanajohnson.com/2012/10/22/desdichado/. (Having never read *Ivanhoe* myself, I owe Johnson a debt of thanks for identifying the origin of the name!)

37. C. S. Lewis [Clive Hamilton, pseud.], "Satan Speaks," *Spirits in Bondage* (London: Heinemann, 1919), http://www.gutenberg.org/files/20 03/2003-h/2003-h.htm.

Chapter 2 "A High Wind"

1. Lewis to the editor of *Encounter*, January 1963, *The Collected Letters of C. S. Lewis*, vol. 3, ed. Walter Hooper, *Narnia, Cambridge, and Joy, 1950–1963* (New York: HarperCollins, 2007), 1400.

2. See editor's note on Lewis to Sayers, October 23, 1942, *Collected Letters of C. S. Lewis*, 2:514.

3. See Phillips, *C. S. Lewis at the BBC*, 203.

4. See Crystal Downing, "Dorothy Sayers Did Not Want to Be a Prophet," *Christianity Today*, May 18, 2018, https://www.christianitytoday .com/ct/2018/june/dorothy-sayers-reluctant-prophet.html.

5. George M. Marsden, *C. S. Lewis's Mere Christianity: A Biography*, in Lives of Great Religious Books series (Princeton: Princeton University Press, 2016), 25.

6. Sayer, *Jack*, 273–74.

7. Lewis, *Surprised by Joy*, 125.

8. Philip Zaleski and Carol Zaleski, *The Fellowship: The Literary Lives of the Inklings* (New York: Farrar, Straus & Giroux, 2015), 176.

9. Lewis to Arthur Greeves, October 18, 1931, *Collected Letters of C. S. Lewis*, 1:977.

10. Lewis, *Surprised by Joy*, 125.

11. See Sayers to the Sister Superior of The Hostel of God, June 25, 1941, *Letters of Dorothy L. Sayers*, 2:265; and Sayers to Amy Davies, November 26, 1941, 2:325, for Sayers's first two mentions of Lewis in her correspondence.

12. See Lewis to Greeves, December 23, 1941, *Collected Letters of C. S. Lewis*, 2:505.

13. J. R. R. Tolkien to Christopher Tolkien, May 25, 1944, *The Letters of J. R. R. Tolkien*, ed. Humphrey Carpenter with Christopher Tolkien (Boston: Houghton Mifflin, 2000), 82.

14. Catherine Kenney, *The Remarkable Case of Dorothy L. Sayers* (Kent, OH: Kent State University Press, 1990), 249.

15. Phillips, *C. S. Lewis at the BBC*, 7.

16. Hooper, editor's note, *Collected Letters of C. S. Lewis*, 2:514.

17. Lewis to Sayers, undated but marked April 1942, *Collected Letters of C. S. Lewis*, 2:515.

18. See Lewis to Arthur Greeves, February 7, 1917, *Collected Letters of C. S. Lewis*, 1: 274, for Lewis's own explanation of the term.

19. Lewis to Mary Van Deusen, *Collected Letters of C. S. Lewis*, 3:108.

20. For details about Bill White and his wife (referred to only as "Mrs. White" by Barbara Reynolds) and about the episode in general, see "Appendix: Particulars of the Birth of John Anthony," in *Letters of Dorothy L. Sayers*, 2:437–41.

21. Sayers to John Cournos, August 22, 1924, *Letters of Dorothy L. Sayers*, 1:216.

22. Sayers to Cournos, 1:217.

23. Sayers, *Strong Poison* (New York: HarperPaperbacks, 1995), 43.

24. Sayers to Ivy Shrimpton, January 27, 1924, *Letters of Dorothy L. Sayers*, 1:208.

25. Reynolds, *Dorothy L. Sayers: Her Life and Soul*, 141–2.

26. Sayers to Cournos, *Letters of Dorothy L. Sayers*, 1:215.

27. Reynolds, *Dorothy L. Sayers: Her Life and Soul*, 154.

28. Dorothy L. Sayers, *Clouds of Witness and The Unpleasantness at the Bellona Club* (New York: Harper & Row, 1970), 196.

29. Lewis to Sayers, undated but marked April 6, 1942, *Collected Letters of C. S. Lewis*, 2:516.

30. Lewis to Sayers, October 23, 1942, *Collected Letters of C. S. Lewis*, 2:533.

31. Christine A. Colón, *Writing for the Masses: Dorothy L. Sayers and the Victorian Literary Tradition*, in Routledge Studies in Twentieth-Century Literature series (New York: Routledge, 2018), 155.

32. Sayers to Lewis, May 13, 1943, *Letters of Dorothy L. Sayers*, 2:410.

33. Sayers to Lewis, May 13, 1943, 2:410.

34. Sayers to Lewis, May 13, 1943, 2:411.

Chapter 3 "Hey! Whoa!"

1. Marjorie Lamp Mead, conversation with the author at the Marion E. Wade Center, January 10, 2018.

2. See Lewis to Sayers, March 18, 1943, *Collected Letters of C. S. Lewis*, 2:564.

3. Lewis to Sayers, May 30(?), 1943, *Collected Letters of C. S. Lewis*, 2:577.

4. Sayers to Lewis, December 3, 1945, *The Letters of Dorothy L. Sayers*, vol. 3, ed. Barbara Reynolds, *A Noble Daring: 1944 to 1950* (Cambridge: The Dorothy L. Sayers Society, 1998), 177.

5. Lewis to Brother George Every, SSM, February 4, 1941, *Collected Letters of C. S. Lewis*, 2:469; Sayers to Barbara Reynolds, December 21, 1955, 4:264.

6. Zaleski and Zaleski, *Fellowship*, 354.

7. Davidman to Chad Walsh, January 27, 1950, *Out of My Bone: The Letters of Joy Davidman*, ed. Don King (Grand Rapids: Eerdmans, 2009), 115.

8. Sayers to Lewis, July 3, 1945, *Letters of Dorothy L. Sayers*, 3:154.

9. Lewis to Sayers, July 6, 1945, *Collected Letters of C. S. Lewis*, 2:663.

10. Sayers to Lewis, July 7, 1945, *Letters of Dorothy L. Sayers*, 3:155.

11. Grevel Lindop, *Charles Williams: The Third Inkling* (New York: Oxford University Press, 2015), 404–5.

12. This letter is not included in Lewis's collected letters, but is quoted by Barbara Reynolds, editor's note in *Letters of Dorothy L. Sayers*, 3:155.

13. Although this should not be discounted. The conflict throws fresh light, for instance, on Jack's famous 1948 debate with Elizabeth Anscombe over his argument, in his book *Miracles*, that naturalism is self-refuting. The common perception has been that Jack felt "defeated" and, consequentially, "spiritually deflated," and he did in fact go back and alter the relevant portion of *Miracles*. But this speculation about his feelings does not seem likely to be true. As Dr. Crystal Hurd points out, simply rethinking his argument was hardly evidence of "resentment," and he continued to interact on a friendly basis with Anscombe and even recommended her as his successor as president of the Oxford Socratic Club. This interpretation seems far likelier to be true when one knows of his friendship with Sayers; any man who had made it through a conflict with her was hardly likely to be thrown by a polite and respectful debate with a young female scholar! For more on the Anscombe-Lewis debate, see Dr. Crystal Hurd, "Iron Sharpens Iron: Elizabeth Anscombe," Week Five in the C. S. Lewis and Women series, July 1, 2013, CrystalHurd.com, http://crystalhurd.com/iron-sharpens-iron-elizabeth-anscombe/.

14. Lewis to Sayers, July 23, 1946, *Collected Letters of C. S. Lewis*, 2:721–22.

15. This letter is not in Sayers's collected letters or in the Marion E. Wade Center, but is mentioned by Barbara Reynolds, editor's note, *Letters of Dorothy L. Sayers*, 3:252.

16. Lewis to Sayers, July 29, 1946, *Collected Letters of C. S. Lewis*, 2:728.

17. "The last temptation is the greatest treason: to do the right deed for the wrong reason." T. S. Eliot, *Murder in the Cathedral*, part I. See note 3, Sayers to Lewis, July 31, 1946, *Letters of Dorothy L. Sayers*, 3:253.

18. Sayers to Lewis, July 31, 1946, 3:253.

19. Sayers to Lewis, July 31, 1946, 3:252–4.

20. Sayers to Lewis, July 31, 1946, 3:254.

21. Lewis to Sayers, August 2, 1946, *Collected Letters of C. S. Lewis*, 2:730.

22. Sayers to Lewis, August 3, 1946, *Letters of Dorothy L. Sayers*, 3:255–57.

23. Lewis to Sayers, August 7, 1946, *Collected Letters of C. S. Lewis*, 2:731.

24. Sayers to Lewis, August 8, 1946, *Letters of Dorothy L. Sayers*, 3:258–60.

25. Lewis to Sayers, December 29, 1946, *Collected Letters of C. S. Lewis*, 2:749.

26. C. S. Lewis, "On Three Ways of Writing for Children," in *On Stories and Other Essays on Literature*, ed. Walter Hooper (San Diego: Harvest/HBJ, 1982), 41–42.

27. Kathleen Lea, "Memories of Lewis as a Colleague," *The Chesterton Review*, vol. 27 no. 4 (November 1991): 400. Emphasis in original.

Chapter 4 "A Complete Blank"

1. Lewis to Sayers, July 13, 1948, *Collected Letters of C. S. Lewis*, 2:860–61.

2. Kathryn Wehr, "Disambiguation: Sayers as a Catholic," *VII: Journal of the Marion E. Wade Center*, vol. 33 (2016): 7–17.

3. Sayers to Lewis, July 19, 1948, *Letters of Dorothy L. Sayers*, 3:387.

4. Reynolds, *Dorothy L. Sayers: Her Life and Soul*, 358.

5. Sayers to Lewis, July 19, 1948, 3:387–88.

6. See Reynolds, *Dorothy L. Sayers: Her Life and Soul*, 354.

7. Lindop, *Charles Williams*, 404.

8. Sayers to Lewis, May 24, 1945, *Letters of Dorothy L. Sayers*, 3:148.

9. Diana Pavlac Glyer, *The Company They Keep: C. S. Lewis and J. R. R. Tolkien as Writers in Community* (Kent, OH: Kent State University Press, 2007), 172.

10. For an in-depth look at Sayers's circle of female friends, see Mo Moulton, *The Mutual Admiration Society: How Dorothy L. Sayers and Her Oxford Circle Remade the World for Women* (New York: Basic Books, 2019).

11. Sayers to Charles Williams, August 16–17, 1944, *Letters of Dorothy L. Sayers*, 3:49.

12. Reynolds, *Dorothy L. Sayers: Her Life and Soul*, 244.

13. Sayers to John Wren-Lewis, March 1954, *Letters of Dorothy L. Sayers*, 4:138.

14. Sayers, *Gaudy Night*, 179–80.

15. Mary Stewart Van Leeuwen, *A Sword between the Sexes?: C. S. Lewis and the Gender Debates* (Grand Rapids: Brazos, 2010), 38.

16. Dorothy L. Sayers, "Are Women Human?" in *Are Women Human?: Astute and Witty Essays on the Role of Women in Society* (Grand Rapids: Eerdmans, 1971), 34.

17. Jacobs, *The Narnian*, 255.

18. Dr. Joy Jordan-Lake, "'She Is One of the Great Ones.' The Radical World of *The Great Divorce*," in *Women and C. S. Lewis: What His Life and Literature Reveal for Today's Culture*, ed. Carolyn Curtis and Mary Pomeroy Key (Oxford: Lion Hudson, 2015), 121.

19. Alister McGrath, "On Tolkien, the Inklings—and Lewis's Blindness to Gender," in *Women and C. S. Lewis*, 83.

20. See Van Leeuwen, *Sword between the Sexes?*, 99 n. 52, in which she points out that Jack and Warren differed on this point.

21. Dr. David Downing, conversation with the author, July 19, 2018.

22. Van Leeuwen, *Sword between the Sexes?*, 37.

23. Van Leeuwen, *Sword between the Sexes?*, 104.

24. See, for instance, his letter to his former pupil Mary Shelley Neylan, quoted by Van Leeuwen in *Sword between the Sexes?*, 118–19.

25. C. S. Lewis, "Membership," in *The Weight of Glory and Other Addresses*, ed. Walter Hooper (New York: Touchstone, 1996), 128.

26. Lewis, "Membership," 128.

27. Lewis, "Membership," 126.

28. Lewis to Margaret Fuller, April 8, 1948, *Collected Letters of C. S. Lewis*, 2:849. See also "Don vs. Devil," *TIME*, September 8, 1947, http://content.time.com/time/subscriber/article/0,33009,804196-1,00.html. Interestingly, Sayers is mentioned in the article as a fellow member of "a whole school of literary evangelists," and quoted at some length on the subject of society's renewed interest in Christianity.

29. Van Leeuwen, *Sword between the Sexes?*, 110.

30. Sayers to John Wren-Lewis, March 1954, *Letters of Dorothy L. Sayers*, 4:143.

31. C. S. Lewis, "Equality," in *Present Concerns*, ed. Walter Hooper (San Diego: Harcourt, 1986), 17.

32. Lewis, "Membership," 128.

33. Byrd, *Why Can't We Be Friends?*, 191.

34. Van Leeuwen, *Sword between the Sexes?*, 255.

35. Lewis, *Four Loves*, 249.

36. Lewis, *Four Loves*, 252.

37. Mead, conversation with the author, January 10, 2018.

38. "Barbara Reynolds, Dante Scholar—Obituary," *The Telegraph*, June 29, 2015, https://www.telegraph.co.uk/news/obituaries/11706348/Barbara-Reynolds-Dante-scholar-obituary.html.

39. The original letter in which Sayers used the term appears to have been lost. But she reiterated the opinion in her next letter to Lewis on August 8, 1955, in *Letters of Dorothy L. Sayers*, 4:253.

40. Lewis to Sayers, August 5, 1955, *Collected Letters of C. S. Lewis*, 3:638–39.

41. Sayers, *Gaudy Night*, 354.

42. Sayers to Reynolds, December 21, 1955, *Letters of Dorothy L. Sayers*, 4:263–64.

43. Dr. Crystal Downing, email to the author, August 27, 2018.

44. Lewis to Sayers, October 23, 1942, *Collected Letters of C. S. Lewis*, 2:534.

45. Sayers to Williams, August 16–17, 1944, *Letters of Dorothy L. Sayers*, 3:45.

46. Sayers to Williams, August 16–17, 1944, 3:48.

47. John Milton, "Book Four, Lines 297–99," *Paradise Lost* (1667), https://www.bartleby.com/4/404.html.

48. Sayers, *Strong Poison*, 44.

49. Sayers to Reynolds, December 21, 1955, *Letters of Dorothy L. Sayers*, 4:264.

50. Sayers to Lewis, August 5, 1946, *Letters of Dorothy L. Sayers*, 3:256.

51. Lewis to Sayers, August 6, 1946, *Collected Letters of C. S. Lewis*, 2:730.

52. Sayers to Lewis, August 8, 1946, *Letters of Dorothy L. Sayers*, 3:260.

53. Sayers to Mrs. Robert Darby, May 31, 1948, *Letters of Dorothy L. Sayers*, 3:375.

54. Sayers to Cournos, October 27, 1924, *Letters of Dorothy L. Sayers*, 1:217–18.

55. Sayers to Lewis, August 12, 1946, in the Marion E. Wade Center collection, accessed January 6, 2018.

56. C. S. Lewis, *A Grief Observed* (New York: Bantam Books, 1976), 56.

57. Lewis to Florence "Michal" Williams, May 22, 1945, *Collected Letters of C. S. Lewis*, 2:653.

58. Sørina Higgins, "An Introduction to Charles Williams," *The Oddest Inkling,* June 5, 2013, https://theoddestinkling.wordpress.com/2013/06/05/intro/.

59. Lindop, *Charles Williams,* 320.

60. Colin Duriez, *Tolkien and C. S. Lewis: The Gift of Friendship* (Mahwah, NJ: HiddenSpring, 2003), 119.

61. Zaleski and Zaleski, *Fellowship,* 269.

62. Sayers to Barbara Reynolds, December 21, 1955, *Letters of Dorothy L. Sayers,* 4:264.

63. Lewis to a Friend, marked [1945?], *Letters of C. S. Lewis,* revised and enlarged ed., ed. W. H. Lewis and Walter Hooper (San Diego: Harcourt Brace & Co.), 380.

64. Sayers to Rev. Dom Christopher Fullman, O.S.B., December 6, 1950, *Letters of Dorothy L. Sayers,* 3:527.

65. Sayers to John Wren-Lewis, marked Good Friday, March 1954 (although Good Friday that year was actually in April), *Letters of Dorothy L. Sayers,* 4:143.

66. As quoted by Reynolds, *Dorothy L. Sayers: Her Life and Soul,* 384, note on page 353.

67. Sayers to Lewis, March 5, 1954, in the Marion E. Wade Center collection, accessed January 6, 2018.

68. Sayers to Lewis, March 5, 1954.

69. Lewis to Sayers, March 9, 1954, *Collected Letters of C. S. Lewis,* 3:437–38.

70. Lindop, *Charles Williams,* 337.

71. Zaleski and Zaleski, *Fellowship,* 282. Brackets are theirs.

72. Zaleski and Zaleski, *Fellowship,* 279.

73. Lewis, *Four Loves,* 255.

74. Mead, conversation with the author, January 10, 2018.

75. Lindop, *Charles Williams,* 404.

76. Lindop, *Charles Williams,* 360.

77. Lewis to Sayers, December 22, 1955 (and footnote from Hooper), *Collected Letters of C. S. Lewis,* 3:690.

78. Lewis to Sayers, November 27, 1955, *Collected Letters of C. S. Lewis,* 3:676.

79. Sayers to Lewis, December 12, 1955, in the Marion E. Wade Center collection, accessed January 6, 2018.

Chapter 5 "Sister Dinosaur"

1. Sayers to Lewis, June 2, 1947, *Letters of Dorothy L. Sayers*, 3:305.

2. Lewis to Sayers, June 5, 1947, *Collected Letters of C. S. Lewis*, 2:779.

3. As quoted by David J. Theroux, "Mere Friendship: Lewis on a Great Joy," *The C. S. Lewis Blog*, July 20, 2009, http://www.cslewis.com/mere-friendship-lewis-on-a-great-joy/.

4. Lewis, *Four Loves*, 248.

5. Lewis to Sayers, June 12, 1954, *Collected Letters of C. S. Lewis*, 3:489.

6. Lewis to Sayers, December 28, 1949, *Collected Letters of C. S. Lewis*, 2:1014.

7. Lewis to Sayers, July 29, 1946; Lewis to Sayers, July 13, 1948; Lewis to Sayers, October 26, 1948; Lewis to Sayers, January 1, 1949; *Collected Letters of C. S. Lewis*, 2:729, 861, 887, and 902.

8. Sayers to Lewis, January 26, 1949, *Letters of Dorothy L. Sayers*, 3:421.

9. Lewis to Sayers, December 16, 1953, *Collected Letters of C. S. Lewis*, 3:387.

10. Barbara Reynolds, editor's note, *Letters of Dorothy L. Sayers*, 4:196.

11. Lewis to Sayers, December 27, 1954, *Collected Letters of C. S. Lewis*, 3:548.

12. Sayers to Lewis, December 29, 1954, *Letters of Dorothy L. Sayers*, 4:198.

13. Lewis to Sayers, January 1, 1949, *Collected Letters of C. S. Lewis*, 2:902.

14. Sayers to Lewis, June 2, 1947, *Letters of Dorothy L. Sayers*, 3:304.

15. Lewis to Sayers, June 12, 1954, *Collected Letters of C. S. Lewis*, 3:488.

16. Duriez, *Tolkien and C. S. Lewis*, 128.

17. Lindop, *Charles Williams*, 309.

18. Lewis to Williams, March 23, 1936, *Collected Letters of C. S. Lewis*, 2:186–87. Quoted by Glyer in *Company They Keep*, 83.

19. See Zaleski and Zaleski, *Fellowship*, 357–59.

20. Glyer, *Company They Keep*, 83–86.

21. Glyer, *Company They Keep*, 378–79.

22. See, for instance, Lewis to Sayers, July 29, 1946, *Collected Letters of C. S. Lewis*, 2:729.

23. Sayers to Reynolds, February 10, 1956, *Letters of Dorothy L. Sayers*, 4:271–72.

24. Lewis to Sayers, July 31, 1955, *Collected Letters of C. S. Lewis*, 3:634.

25. As quoted by Hooper, *Collected Letters of C. S. Lewis*, 3:634 n. 230.

26. Sayers to Lewis, December 12, 1955, *The Letters of Dorothy L. Sayers*, 4:262.

27. Dr. Crystal Downing, "The Divine Comedy of C. S. Lewis and Dorothy L. Sayers," in *Women and C. S. Lewis*, 74. See also Sayers to Lewis, January 26, 1949, *Letters of Dorothy L. Sayers*, 3:421.

28. Lewis to Sayers, November 11, 1949, *Collected Letters of C. S. Lewis*, 2:996.

29. Sayers to Lewis, November 18, 1949, *Letters of Dorothy L. Sayers*, 4:465.

30. Lewis to Sayers, November 22, 1954, *Collected Letters of C. S. Lewis*, 3:529.

31. Ian Thomson, "A Grand Tour in the Circles of Hell: Ian Thomson Considers the History of Dante's Masterpiece and a Lively New Translation," *The Independent*, February 26, 1994, https://www.independent.co.uk/arts-entertainment/books/book-review-a-grand-tour-in-the-circles-of-hell-ian-thomson-considers-the-history-of-dantes-1396477.html.

32. Sayers to John Anthony Fleming, June 14, 1950, *Letters of Dorothy L. Sayers*, 3:509.

33. Sayers to Muriel St. Clare Byrne, June 12, 1950, *Letters of Dorothy L. Sayers*, 3:508.

34. Lewis to Greeves, June 15, 1950, *Collected Letters of C. S. Lewis*, 3:37–8.

35. Lewis to Sayers, March 4, 1954, *Collected Letters of C. S. Lewis*, 3:435.

36. Lewis to Sayers, September 25, 1954, *Collected Letters of C. S. Lewis*, 3:508.

37. Zaleski and Zaleski, *Fellowship*, 341.

38. Kathleen Nott, *The Emperor's Clothes: An Attack on the Dogmatic Orthodoxy of T. S. Eliot, Graham Greene, Dorothy Sayers, C. S. Lewis, and Others* (Bloomington: Indiana University Press, 1958), 33–34, archived at http://archive.org/details/emperorsclothes00nott.

39. Dorothy L. Sayers, "A Debate Deferred, Part I: The Dogma in the Manger: A Reply to Kathleen Nott," in *VII: An Anglo-American Literary Review*, vol. 3 (1982): 37.

40. Nott, *Emperor's Clothes*, 254.

41. Sayers to Reynolds, July 25, 1956, *Letters of Dorothy L. Sayers*, 4:318.

42. Lewis to Sayers, December 16, 1953, *Collected Letters of C. S. Lewis*, 3:387.

43. Sayers to Lewis, December 21, 1953, *Letters of Dorothy L. Sayers*, 4:117.

44. Sayers to R. Stephen Talmage, April 12, 1954, *Letters of Dorothy L. Sayers*, 4:153.

45. John Wren-Lewis, "The Chester-Lewis," *The Chesterton Review*, vol. 27 no. 4 (November 1991): 564.

46. Sayers, "Debate Deferred," 44.

47. Duriez, *Tolkien and C. S. Lewis*, 148–51.

48. Sayers to Reynolds, December 7, 1954, *Letters of Dorothy L. Sayers*, 4:186.

49. Duriez, *Tolkien and C. S. Lewis*, 153.

50. Lewis, "De Descriptione Temporum: Inaugural Lecture from the Chair of Mediaeval and Renaissance Literature at Cambridge University, 1954," Internet Archive, accessed January 8, 2020, https://archive.org/details/DeDescriptioneTemporum/page/n0.

51. Sayers to Lewis, April 4, 1955, *Letters of Dorothy L. Sayers*, 4:222–23.

52. Lewis to Sayers, April 6, 1955, *Collected Letters of C. S. Lewis*, 3:596.

53. Lewis to Sayers, July 1, 1957, *Collected Letters of C. S. Lewis*, 3:863.

54. Tolkien, as quoted in Glyer, *Company They Keep*, 84.

55. Zaleski and Zaleski, *Fellowship*, 378.

56. Zaleski and Zaleski, *Fellowship*, 378.

57. Davidman to Chad Walsh, December 13, 1954, *Out of My Bone*, 228.

Chapter 6 "I Do Most Heartily Rejoice"

1. C. S. Lewis, "A Panegyric for Dorothy L. Sayers," in *On Stories and Other Essays on Literature*, 91.

2. Davidman to William Lindsay Gresham, October 29, 1954, *Out of My Bone*, 223.

3. Lewis and Davidman to Sayers, August 9, 1955, *Collected Letters of C. S. Lewis*, 3:641.

4. Duriez, *Tolkien and C. S. Lewis*, 160–61.

5. Van Leeuwen, *Sword between the Sexes?*, 107.

6. Lyle W. Dorsett, "Helen Joy Davidman (Mrs. C. S. Lewis) 1915–1960: A Portrait," C. S. Lewis Institute, accessed October 7, 2018, http://www.cslewisinstitute.org/node/31.

7. Lewis to Sayers, December 24, 1956, *Collected Letters of C. S. Lewis*, 3:819.

8. Lewis, *Four Loves*, 250.

9. Sayers to Anthony Fleming, December 16, 1949, *Letters of Dorothy L. Sayers*, 3:473.

10. Jacobs, *Narnian*, 278.

11. Lewis to Sayers, June 25, 1957, *Collected Letters of C. S. Lewis*, 3:861.

12. Lewis to Sayers, June 25, 1957, 3:861–62.

13. Lewis to Sayers, July 1, 1957, *Collected Letters of C. S. Lewis*, 3:863.

14. Sayers to Reynolds, September 5, 1956, *Letters of Dorothy L. Sayers*, 4:328.

15. Lewis, *Four Loves*, 269.

16. Lewis to Sayers, June 25, 1957, *Collected Letters of C. S. Lewis*, 3:862.

17. Lewis to Sayers, July 1, 1957, 3:864.

18. Jacobs, *Narnian*, 285.

19. Sayers to Lewis, July 3, 1957, in the Marion E. Wade Center collection, accessed January 10, 2018.

Chapter 7 "A Friend, Not an Ally"

1. Lewis, "Panegyric for Dorothy L. Sayers," 94.

2. Crystal Downing and David C. Downing, "Douglas Gresham Interview—Part 3," *The Wade Center Podcast*, season 1, episode 1, Marion E. Wade Center, December 6, 2018, http://wheaton.edu/listen/wade-center-podcast. Douglas Gresham reiterated this story when I met him in person at The C. S. Lewis Influence and Relevance Today conference in Montreat, North Carolina, November 2019. See also Glyer, *Company They Keep*, 23, n. 21: "[Joy] Davidman's son Douglas Gresham has noted, 'Dorothy Sayers and Jack (and my mother) were good friends, and one of the rare times I saw Jack deeply upset (other than his grief for my mother) was when he received the news that Dorothy had died' (MereLewis Listserve Archives, 27 June 1996 14:47:41)."

3. Byrd, *Why Can't We Be Friends?*, 176.

4. Anthony Fleming, as quoted in Reynolds, *Dorothy L. Sayers: Her Life and Soul*, 346.

5. Reynolds, *Dorothy L. Sayers: Her Life and Soul*, 244.

6. Hooper, preface, in C. S. Lewis, *On Stories and Other Essays in Literature*, xx.

7. Hooper, editor's note, in *Collected Letters of C. S. Lewis*, 3:915.

8. Lewis to Fleming, January 21, 1958, *Collected Letters of C. S. Lewis*, 3:915.

9. Lewis, "Panegyric for Dorothy L. Sayers," 91.

10. Lewis, "Panegyric for Dorothy L. Sayers," 91–92.

11. Lewis, "Panegyric for Dorothy L. Sayers," 92.

12. Lewis, "Panegyric for Dorothy L. Sayers," 92.

13. Lewis, "Panegyric for Dorothy L. Sayers," 92.

14. See Sayers to Lewis, August 12, 1946, in the Marion E. Wade Center collection, accessed January 6, 2018.

15. Lewis, "Panegyric for Dorothy L. Sayers," 93.

16. Lewis, "Panegyric for Dorothy L. Sayers," 93.

17. Lewis, "Panegyric for Dorothy L. Sayers," 95.

18. See Lewis to Fleming, January 21, 1958, *Collected Letters of C. S. Lewis*, 3:915.

19. Lewis to the editor of *Encounter*, January 1963, *Collected Letters of C. S. Lewis*, 3:1400.

20. Lewis to Charles Moorman, May 15, 1959, *Collected Letters of C. S. Lewis*, 3:1049.

21. Lewis to Charles Moorman, May 15, 1959, 3:1049.

22. Glyer, *Company They Keep*, 71.

23. Lewis to Sayers, July 31, 1955, *Collected Letters of C. S. Lewis*, 3:635.

24. Sherwood Wirt, "An Interview with C. S. Lewis," *Decision* (September 1963), accessed October 2, 2018, https://bensonian.files.wordpress.com/2012/04/interview.pdf.

25. Dorothy L. Sayers, "The King Comes to His Own," Scene One, the twelfth play in *The Man Born to Be King* (San Francisco: Ignatius Press, 1990), 319.

26. Sayers, "The King Comes to His Own," Scene One.

27. Sayers, "The Human-Not-Quite-Human" in *Are Women Human?*, 68.

28. Sayers to Brother George Every, SSM, July 10, 1947, *Letters of Dorothy L. Sayers*, 3:315.

Gina Dalfonzo is a writer who has been published in *The Atlantic*, *Christianity Today*, *The Weekly Standard*, *Guideposts*, *Aleteia*, and *OnFaith*, among others. She is the author of *One by One: Welcoming the Singles in Your Church* (Baker Books, 2017). She is also a columnist at *Christ and Pop Culture* and the founder and editor of *Dickensblog*. She earned her BA in English from Messiah College and her MA, also in English, from George Mason University. Dalfonzo lives in Springfield, Virginia.